Contents

Foreword

Although every effort may be made by careers advisers to convey information about courses to potential students there are, inevitably, gaps in the available information and many unanswered questions.

In this book Sheila Herrman spells out in some detail the range of opportunities open to nursery nurses in training, the requirements of the course, and the kinds of skills that need to be developed. Potential students will come to understand what will be expected of them if they decide to apply to train as a nursery nurse. Students at the start of their course will find this book may help them to understand the seeming complexity of the programme upon which they are embarking. Careers advisers will find it an invaluable addition to their resources.

Sheila Herrman has had many years of experience with young children and with nursery nurse students in training. This book fills a gap in the available literature on nursery nursing. It will be warmly welcomed.

BARBARA MOGFORD BREAKELL

Director of Courses
The National Nursery Examination Board

Preface

An Introduction to Nursery Nursing is planned, primarily, for students about to start nursery nurse training. The topics covered are those which tutors need to discuss during the induction of students into the course, and which will be referred to by them frequently through the first year of the NNEB training. (Although I have referred throughout to the nursery nurse student as female, it should be mentioned that young men are also allowed to qualify as nursery nurses and there are now a few male NNEB Certificate holders.)

There will be no attempt to cover the vocational Child Development and Health curriculum of the course, as this is adequately provided for in a number of publications.

There remains, however, an area of vocational guidance which is as yet uncovered by other texts. This includes advice and help with particular details unique to the NNEB course and its organisation. It is very important, for example, that the complete training be understood by those concerned, as too often students have disconnected ideas about nursery nursing which they find difficult to see as a whole. An overall picture of the training from start to finish will assist students in setting themselves goals and understanding their own aims.

It is hoped that those considering nursery nursing as a possible training will find this publication a help in deciding on their future career.

Acknowledgements

This book has been written as a result of my work with children and students over a number of years. The infinite variety of these individual children and young people has provided me with a constant stimulus as a practising teacher, and I am grateful for the many happy experiences I have gained in their company. The teaching profession has also provided me with a never-ending source of friends and colleagues who have helped me with kindness and support whenever I have needed it.

In Warwickshire I have been particularly fortunate in finding a warm welcome in whatever college or school I have visited and I would like to thank particularly the principals, head teachers, and staff of all those schools and colleges with which I am concerned.

I wish to thank Miss B. Wright, Chairman of the NNEB, and the Board, for their permission to publish given information and the syllabus as an appendix. Mrs. Mogford Breakell, Director of Courses at the NNEB, has been extremely kind and I am most grateful to her for reading the original manuscript and offering sound advice and help towards its improvement.

Miss Mary Cortis of ILEA provided me with up-to-date information about recent developments in the provision for children in London.

My thanks for permission to have photographs taken go to the Coventry Maternity Hospital; Warnford Hospital (Maternity Unit), Leamington Spa; Weddington First School, Nuneaton; Warwick Nursery School, Warwick; Lillington Nursery School, Leamington Spa; and Bedworth Heath Nursery School, Bedworth. All these photographs and those on the cover were taken by Simon Butler of Simon Browne, Leamington Spa.

The Church of England Children's Society have provided a photograph of a residential home (Plate 4), as well as information about their work, for which I am most grateful. Dr. Barnardo's have also kindly provided information. Permission to print information from *Social Trends* in Table 1 has been granted by HMSO.

Lastly I would like to thank my son Colin, whose drawings for cartoons have proved useful, and whose help and encouragement I constantly receive.

SHEILA HERRMAN
October 1978

I

The Work of the Nursery Nurse

So you want to be a nursery nurse?

One of the things you will study if you train to be a nursery nurse is child development. We know from studies of development that teenage girls between 14 and 16 have a strong interest in children, and this is quite a reasonable occurrence as they begin to think of themselves as future mothers and are excited at such a prospect.

It is not uncommon, therefore, for young girls to be attracted to working with children. If you feel this interest yourself, now might be a good time to ask: what have I based this decision on? Do I know many children? Have I ever been with them in a group? Have I spent a great deal of time with them? Questions like this might reveal that your real experience of children is very limited, and it might follow that in your thoughts about children you have an unrealistic image of pretty darlings who need cuddling. Then you might wonder if it is indeed your own need to cuddle a lovely young child which is making you think of working with children. If this is so it would be wise to set out systematically to try to gain some actual experience. This may not be easy, but in this way you will eventually attain a wider understanding of children, which is necessary for such an important decision. When you have looked after children who are poorly and fractious, rude and dirty, and you are tired out, then is the time to ask yourself again: do I want to work with children? If the answer is still yes, then the work you have chosen will be one of the most rewarding careers you could select.

Although a liking for and an interest in children is, of course, an important prerequisite to starting a nursery nurse training scheme, you will find that many other qualities are needed which are just as important.

Since virtually all work with children involves at least the child's parents or other staff wherever you work, it is vitally important that you get on well with other people. At a young age your experience with friends may be all you have to go on when thinking about getting on with people at work. As you progress through training and become more mature yourself, you will need to be able to meet adults in working situations and adjust yourself where necessary. This may seem an easy and obvious task, which can be overlooked and taken for granted. In fact, getting on with others is a skill which should be seen as something to work at continually, and must include a wide span of people from the bus conductor to colleagues at work, as well as friends and relatives. You will find that during your course you will be required to get on with a very large number of people in very different situations, and this in itself is an essential part of the training.

College entry requirements

There is no stated entry requirement from NNEB about students commencing training courses. Colleges decide on their own requirements, and this varies, from a general academic ability which would indicate they could benefit from study and training, to three or four GCE 'O' level or equivalent passes before beginning the course. Since this is a popular course, and most colleges have many more applicants than they can accept, they are able to select students not only on academic ability but more importantly on personality and suitability to work with children. This usually means that applicants are interviewed and a request is made to the applicant's school for a reference. One of the important questions to be asked is whether applicants are reliable and trustworthy and, therefore, to be trusted with the care of young children.

It is possible that NNEB will soon decide on a specific academic entry requirement in the near future in order to standardise college entry. Arguments put forward against this include the fact that many young girls who are not necessarily very academic may have special qualities and gifts which enable them to contribute greatly in work where they care for young children.

What does a nursery nurse do?

A nursery nurse is trained to know everything about the young child from birth to the age of 7. Her knowledge is built up during training through study, observation and practical experience with children. This practical experience takes place under the guidance of trained staff, so that you as a student are able to see how to handle the children and learn from others more experienced than yourself. During training a big effort is made to give you the experience of working with children in a number of different situations, in order that you should be prepared for the great variety of places that the qualified nursery nurse can find herself working in. Once you have completed your training you are, in short, someone who is trained to meet all the needs of young children, to care for and educate them in the fullest sense of the word. The places in which you might work include the following: local education authority schools and nursery centres; day nurseries and residential institutions run by departments of social services (you could also work under the auspices of these departments as a home visitor or child minder); hospitals; private employment – as a nanny, in private nurseries and schools, with holiday organisations or families abroad, with industrial and university crèches; voluntary organisations.

Working in local education authority schools

The Department of Education and Science recognises the National Nursery Examination Board (NNEB) Certificate as a qualification for employment in education, and local education authorities employ qualified nursery nurses to work in their schools. This work normally involves staff in being at school half an hour before and after the children. They also usually come to school before and after the school year in order to make plans and prepare for the children, as well as attending school functions in the evening or staff meetings whenever called. Staff in schools usually work school hours and have school holidays.

The salary of the nursery assistant in schools takes the longer holidays and shorter hours into account, so that she may be paid less than a nursery nurse employed in a day nursery.

Nursery schools

Nursery assistants are employed in nursery schools and are usually equal in number to the teachers in the school. In this capacity the nursery nurse and teacher work rather like a doctor and nurse team in a hospital. The teacher is responsible for the overall education of the children, and the nursery nurse assists her in every way possible. This assistance will range from the physical care and supervision of the children and classrooms to the provision of a suitable programme for the developmental needs of the children. This partnership is usually a happy and successful one, as each realises the importance and special skills of the other.

Infant and first schools — nursery classes and infant classes

Nursery nurses are employed as assistants in nursery classes attached to primary schools. There will usually be only a small number of children of pre-school age provided for. The nursery nurse works alongside a teacher as a member of the larger school staff.

Nursery nurses are also sometimes employed as 'helpers' in infant and first schools. Their work is to assist the class teacher. It is likely that because of the more formal demands of the educational curriculum at this stage, the nursery nurse will be more involved with the practical side of classroom management and the physical needs of the children. Her caring role may often require her to mother the children. But she will also assist in the educational activities of the classroom. Her role will vary depending on whether the school is organised on formal or informal lines.

Special schools

In the field of special education nursery nurses are much sought after. They may work as helpers in schools for the educationally sub-normal, the partially hearing and the physically handicapped. In fact they can work in any type of special school where their skills are required. In these situations the nursery nurse's understanding of the needs and development of the normal child will fit her to deal sympathetically and patiently with the particular difficulties of the children she is working with. In special schools the nursery nurse works with teachers and sometimes with medical staff.

Nursery centres

In the last ten years there has been a new development in the provision made for pre-school children. This has been the nursery centre. This type of establishment has been set up, and is sometimes run jointly, by the local education authority and the department of social services. The nursery centre combines both nursery school and day care provision under one roof, and this gives a degree of flexibility in the programme offered for the needs of individual parents and children.

The centres do not close for the school holidays, so that working parents are not faced with the problem of providing alternative care for certain periods of the year. Some children attend only in the normal school terms, and may also attend daily for only two or three hours, while others stay from early in the morning until after tea. Clearly, this provision requires very good accommodation and staffing. The combination of services also results in teachers and nursery nurses working together closely as a team providing for all the needs of the children.

The success of these centres has been encouraging, and authorities are seeking ways of extending similar provision for pre-school children in the school holidays. The Inner London Education Authority (ILEA) and the social services departments of the Inner London boroughs are discussing ways of providing care for children who attend full-time nursery provision when the nursery class is closed, i.e., outside school hours, including holiday periods. Although the ILEA cannot spend money on 'day care', accommodation and provisions which become available due to falling school rolls can be used in co-operation with the social services, which are responsible for staffing and running costs. Experimental schemes, such as holiday play centres for 3 – 5-year-olds and care after school for children attending nursery classes, are being set up initially.

Such examples of co-operation are indications of a growing concern for the need for a concerted effort to provide an overall service for families with young children, rather than a number of departmentalised and separate services.

Working for the department of social services

The Department of Health and Social Security also recognises the NNEB Certificate as a qualification, and the local departments of social services employ nursery nurses in a variety of capacities.

Day Nurseries

Nursery nurses are employed in day nurseries where young children are cared for all day when it is impossible for them to stay in their own homes. The nurseries are run and staffed by nursery nurses who are called Nursery Officers. There are also domestic staff employed in the nurseries. The hours of opening are longer than the school day, and can be from as early as 7 a.m. to as late as 7 p.m. This involves staff in shift work, as some start early and others finish late, usually taking turns. They also require adequate breaks during the day. Day nurseries stay open most of the year, closing only for public holidays and sometimes for two or three additional weeks during the year, according to local needs.

Day nurseries can care for children from early infancy up until the age of starting school. Such a large age range requires particularly careful planning to provide appropriately for each age group. Buildings and facilities are strictly governed and the number of staff to children is specified, so that the children have plenty of attention. The Certificate of Nursery Nursing is the most common qualification held by staff working with the children in day nurseries. Such work carries great responsibility and well-trained and experienced nursery nurses are, therefore, of paramount importance to the success of such establishments.

Recent developments in day nursery programmes have seen a change in organisation. In the past different age groups were strictly segregated, so that infants, toddlers and pre-school children were in separate rooms. The programme now takes the form of a family approach, so that children mix much more with different age groups, although infants might be separate for some of the day when they are sleeping. New day nursery buildings are designed with a number of small family rooms and a larger area where the children can all play together if they wish.

Residential care

It is the increasing practice of authorities to try to keep very young children from institutional residential care. It is much better if children can live in normal homes as foster children. Many large residential homes which used to cater for the care of children have now, therefore, been closed down, and the old-fashioned image of the 'orphanage' has certainly disappeared. There are still some establishments, however, which do assume the care of very young babies and children. Staff in these homes do an excellent job of making the buildings as homely as possible, and by keeping the children in small family groups they try to ensure as 'normal' a situation as possible. But the nursery nurses who form part of the staff in these homes need time off, and so there must be fairly frequent changes among the people caring for the children. The nursery nurse has to be prepared to work in shifts.

It is sometimes the case that handicapped babies and children cannot be placed in foster homes because of their special needs. There are a number of residential establishments, therefore, which cater particularly for these children.

Home visiting

This is a new area of work in which nursery nurses have become involved. With the special attention and help which the government has given to areas considered socially and educationally deprived, new methods have been tried to help families with special needs. It has been found that the influence of the mother is vital in the performance of her children as they grow up — not only their general ability in coping with life but also their attitude and performance at school. Where parents have received a poor start in life themselves it is often the case that they do not understand how to help their own young children. A nursery nurse may be employed as a 'home visitor' in these circumstances and her aim will be to encourage the mother and father to talk and play with their babies. Teachers and social workers are also sometimes employed in this way. The work is very demanding on understanding and skill, and it is important that the parents accept these visits as help from a friendly person. If the home visitor is seen as a patronising intruder from the local authority she will obviously have little success. Employment in this capacity is limited, partly due to lack of money and partly due to the novelty of such an approach. Where this work does exist is in the urban conurbations where there is particular need.

Child minding

To look after children daily in your own home you need to be registered with the local social services department. Although you do not have to be a qualified nursery nurse in order to register and do this work, it is obviously an advantage to be qualified. Many authorities do try to give training courses to their child minders. This work has the advantage that it can be done in your own home and if you have your own young children, it can fit in well with your own family's needs.

Working in hospitals

The health authorities and hospital boards accept the NNEB Certificate as qualification to work with children in hospitals.

All work in hospitals involves working in shifts and working with state registered nurses and midwives.

Maternity units

Nursery nurses are often employed in maternity wards to help to look after the babies while mothers are recovering. This involves feeding and bathing the babies as well as helping mothers who are starting to nurse (Plates 1, 2 and 3).

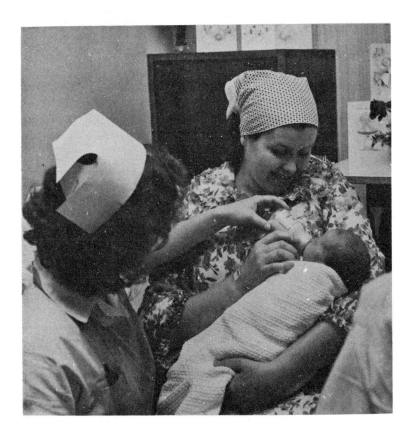

Plate 1. A qualified nursery nurse at Coventry Maternity Hospital helping a new mother to hold the bottle at exactly the right angle for the baby.

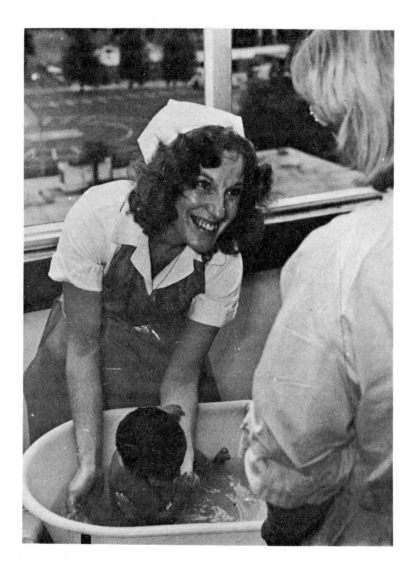

Plate 2. Bathing a new baby.

Plate 3. Weighing a new baby as a midwife staff nurse looks on.

Special-care baby units

Large hospitals have units where newborn babies can receive special care when needed. These babies are usually in incubators and need to be watched carefully and continuously. Nursery nurses are often employed in these units.

Children's wards

Nursery nurses can also work in children's wards in hospitals. Their work involves the caring and mothering role which young children need if they are in hospital without their mothers.

It is important to children's recovery to allow them to play when they are ill, and so a nursery nurse is often the person who provides for play on the children's ward. She has the added attraction of not being the person who administers injections! Depending on the age of the children and the generosity of the staffing, her work will vary a great deal but will certainly include helping with feeding, washing and dressing the children.

Special hospitals

There are some babies and young children who are so severely handicapped that they need care in special hospitals. These hospitals employ nursery nurses to work with the children.

Private employment

Working in the private sector

Although the majority of nursery nurses find work in public employment, in the education, social and health services, in the past few years there have been signs that the pattern of employment is changing and that more nursery nurses are finding work in the private sector. One such indication is the number of daily advertisements for posts for qualified nursery nurses in the national and local press.

Work as a nanny

Married women are increasingly finding that they want or need to return to work when their children are still young and are employing help at home to take care of their children.

In addition, there is a large increase in the numbers of one-parent families and these, too, often need help with the children if the parent is to go to work.

Families with a handicapped child also sometimes employ a nursery nurse to help to take care of the child in the daytime and relieve them of some of the work that such a child incurs.

In these types of posts the nursery nurse attends on a daily basis and usually has flexible hours which are worked out to suit both the family and herself. It may be that she will stay later some evenings to babysit. This could be treated as over-time, or she may be given time off at another time to compensate her instead.

The smaller modern house does not always afford sufficient accommodation for the nursery nurse, but there are still very many posts for live-in nannies advertised.

The relationship between the parent and nanny must be worked out satisfactorily so that all concerned are happy with the arrangement. This will ensure that the child is well cared for and will flourish. It is wise, therefore, to establish from the outset exactly what duties will be yours and which do not apply to your post. Ask about all the details of your work. You will need to know about the hours you are expected to work and the amount of pay you will receive. (It is wise to discuss future possible adjustments in pay if you should stay for more than a year.) Discuss with the parents how they wish the child to be treated and consider carefully before you agree to take a job with a family. In this way you should be able to make a fair judgement about whether you can get on and work with the family.

Once you are working in a family situation you will need to remember the feelings of the parents about their child and make every effort to work with them in wholehearted co-operation. No mother wants to feel she is being replaced in her child's affections, but naturally the child will become attached to the person who cares for him.

The modern-day nanny is very different from the old-fashioned nanny of yesteryear. She works with the family, often in a situation where she shares the full-time duties of caring for young children with parents who work. She is no longer treated as a domestic servant, and parents will try to establish a good working relationship with the nanny, as they know how important this is for their child.

Although there has been this social change, it is still possible that a nanny might feel an 'outsider' within the family, so it is important that a nursery nurse should take care in deciding with whom she will work in this capacity. This type of work often offers good opportunity for travel as the British nanny has a good reputation worldwide.

Private nurseries and schools

There are a number of nurseries and schools run privately by individuals or groups. The work varies greatly according to the establishment and might involve residential or day work.

The holiday industry

More and more package holidays offer special programmes for children in order to allow the parents the freedom to relax. The nursery nurse is well suited to this work and is often employed in this country and abroad. She supervises children and makes sure they are happily provided for in all ways during the holiday. It is likely that this work will be seasonal.

Industrial and university crèches

Some factories and universities provide a crèche where babies can be looked after while the parents work or study. These are run on similar lines to a day nursery or nursery school and usually nursery nurses staff them. The parents can expect to contribute something to the cost of this care, but it is often supplemented by the organisers themselves, who provide accommodation and equipment.

Opportunities for working abroad

Nannying jobs in other countries are frequently available for qualified nursery nurses. It is even more important to take care, in considering such a post, that the family you are going to work with will accept you and that you will be happy with them. Any financial arrangements need to be looked into carefully in order to safeguard your position.

If you have a contract, take care that it is legal in the country which you are going to. Keep your passport safely and don't give it to your employer to keep for you. You can register with the British Embassy and they will hold your passport for you if you wish. It might be wise, also, to have a return ticket available, so that if you need to return home, this is easily possible.

When you consider a job abroad it is even more necessary to find out about the working conditions. Ensure that you have an exact job description before you go, so that there are no mis-understandings after you arrive. Check what salary you are to get and at what rate of exchange. You will need medical insur-ance and you will certainly need to be prepared to learn the language of the country you go to if it is a non-English-speaking country.

If you take all these things into consideration before you go and are prepared for all contingencies, then there will undoub-tedly be many very exciting opportunities and experiences for you as a nursery nurse working abroad as a nanny.

It may also be possible to find employment working with young children in groups in other countries, as most now have various provisions for pre-school children and our membership of the Common Market is making employment of nationals of member countries more possible. There is as yet, however, no formal recognition of our nursery nursing certificate in other countries.

Non-English-speaking countries sometimes welcome an English-speaking nursery nurse to work with young children for whom English is being promoted as a second language. If you yourself have a second language, this obviously would make such prospects very much more likely.

Working for voluntary organisations

There are a number of voluntary organisations which employ nursery nurses. These are generally charitable organisations set up to provide help where it is most needed.

Dr Barnardo's Homes, the Church of England Children's Society, the Save the Children Fund and Father Hudson's Homes are some of those whose names are well known. Most of these have a tradition of providing refuge and residential care for children. The type of care needed has changed in recent years and these organisations have therefore adapted to the new demands, responding to the inner-city need for day care centres and providing care for handicapped children (Plate 4).

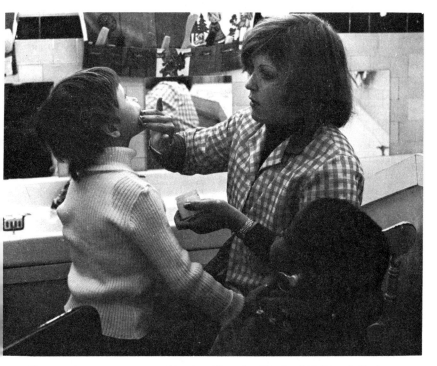

Plate 4. A nursery nurse working in a Church of England Children's Society residential home — watched by a hearing-impaired child.

The Church of England Children's Society employs fifty-one NNEB qualified nursery nurses in ten day care centres for under-5s, and a further eleven in their two residential nurseries for the physically handicapped. Dr Barnardo's, too, employ qualified nursery nurses in its fifteen day care centres and in residential homes for the handicapped. Dr Barnardo's have five establishments in Australia and two in New Zealand. The Save the Children Fund has opened day care centres in the inner cities and works internationally to assist poor children in emergencies such as famine.

Essential qualities to acquire as a nursery nurse

As you can see from the description above of the different kinds of work which nursery nurses can be involved in, one of the prime requirements of a nursery nurse is that she be adaptable. The basic skills and knowledge acquired during training will stand you in good stead, but we all continue to learn as we work in new situations and with new people. It would be a great mistake to believe that at the completion of your training as a nursery nurse you know all there is to know about children and how you will work with them.

It is also wise to keep an open mind about where you will eventually work. It would be foolish to decide firmly that you wished only to work in one of the jobs outlined in this chapter. It may be that the opportunity for that particular work will not be there when you complete your training. Instead, be prepared to try any situation and to move to wherever an interesting job is offered. This is especially important when you first complete your training, as once you have had experience as a qualified nursery nurse, your employment prospects will always be better for the future. If you enjoy working with children you should be able to fit in anywhere.

Table 1 will give you some idea of the number of young children who have been cared for under various services in England and Wales in recent years.

Table 1. Children's services in England and Wales

		Thousands	
		1975	1976
Child health centres (total children attending)		1,729	1,749
Maintained day nurseries (local authority and voluntary bodies)		26	27
Registered nurseries (including most pre-school playgroups)		370	396
Registered child minders		87	85
Nursery education (number of children aged 2 and under 5 in nursery schools and other schools, excluding special schools)			
Maintained primary schools	full-time	305	321
	part-time	95	117
Maintained nursery schools	full-time	15	15
	part-time	33	35
Independent schools	full-time	17	17
	part-time	13	12
Total	full-time	337	353
	part-time	141	164

Source: *Social Trends*, HMSO, 1977.

Questions

1. What qualities and abilities does a student need in order to become a good nursery nurse?

2. What are some of the conditions which might result in a pre-school child spending some time each day away from his own home?

3. How can a qualified nursery nurse work in a local education authority school?

4. Some work with children entails employment by the local department of social services. Where would this type of work take place?

5. Nursery nurses are employed in a variety of situations other than in education and the social services. Describe some of these and discuss how the work will differ according to the situation.

II

The Two-year Course of Training

Background of the NNEB training and its development

During the Second World War, as the men went away women were called upon to take over the work left to do at home. In order to free them for this work, arrangements were made to look after their babies and young children in day nurseries. The then Ministry of Health organised and supervised this provision.

In November 1943 the Royal Sanitary Institute (which is now known as the Royal Society of Health) was asked by the Minister of Health if an examination could be arranged which would be open to all nursery nurses in training. Prior to this several different organisations had issued certificates in nursery nursing, including the National Society of Children's Nurseries and the National Council of Associated Children's Homes (the latter is now the National Council of Voluntary Child Care Organisations).

In January 1944 a meeting was held at which it was resolved to set up a special examination board to administer an examination for all nursery nurses. The National Nursery Examination Board was formed and its first meeting was held in July 1945. The first examination took place in 1946.

The courses of training for nursery nurses which were already running continued to be approved for entry to the NNEB examination until the new training schemes were fully established. There has been rapid growth in the number of candidates since 1947, the first full NNEB course year, when there were 680. Thirty years later, in 1977, there were 5,535 candidates (Table 2).

Table 2. Numbers of NNEB examination candidates 1973–9

1973	1974	1975	1976	1977	1978	1979
					(Projected numbers)	
3443	3941	4950	5384	5535	5235	5534

Source: NNEB

There have been many changes in the training over the years, most notable of which was the extension of the age range of children studied. Originally nursery nurses were trained to care for children from birth to 5 years of age. In 1965 it was decided to extend this to 7. This decision was prompted by the increasing use of classroom assistants in primary schools and the Plowden Report's recommendation that persons trained in working with children should be used for this task. In 1975 the Bullock Report, *A Language for Life*, again recommended that nursery nurses should be used as trained assistants alongside teachers in helping language development in the young child.

Another factor which has influenced the training has been the vast amount of information about children and how they develop which has been rapidly acquired during those thirty years. A great deal more is known now about young children and their needs than in the early part of this century. Research into child development has provided new information about the intellectual, linguistic and emotional development of children, as well as their physical development. There has been rapid social change, which has seen changing patterns of family life and immigration resulting in the development of a multi-ethnic society. Increasing numbers of handicapped children now survive infancy because of better medical care and great strides have been made in the field of medicine through the discovery and use of antibiotics.

These factors have affected the emphasis of the training, which was initially very much on the health of the baby and young child. Today we are, of course, still very concerned to promote excellent health and physical development, but we are also aware of the child's need for stimulation to develop mentally, emotionally and socially.

The NNEB syllabus has been extended so that all this important and necessary information is included in the nursery nurse training. In 1974 the Board decided to extend the theoretical period of training from two to three days a week to allow sufficient time for study of the extended syllabus. The emphasis is now more on the theoretical content of the training than previously. This was seen as an essential change in view of the ever-growing diversity of situations in which the nursery nurse is now employed, and the increasing social complexity of settings in which children are to be found needing care.

The NNEB today

The National Nursery Examination Board is today an entirely independent organisation. It receives no government funds. The Board is made up of representatives from various groups who each nominate a member. The full Board meets three times each year. During 1976 twenty-five meetings were held by the Board, its committees (Finance, Advisory, Examinations) and working parties.

Nominating bodies

Association of County Councils
Association of Directors of Social Services
Association of Education Committees
Association of Metropolitan Authorities
Association of Nursery Training Colleges
British Association for Early Childhood Education
British Association of Social Workers
British Paediatric Association
Central Council for Education and Training in Social Work
Council of Local Education Authorities
Health Visitors Association
National Association of Certified Nursery Nurses
National Association of Head Teachers
National Association of Inspectors and Educational Advisers

National Association of Nursery Matrons
National Association of Teachers in Further and Higher Education
National Association of Tutors in Education and Health (NNEB)
National Council of Voluntary Child Care Organisation
National Union of Teachers
Regional Health Authorities
Residential Care Association
Royal College of Nursing
Royal Society of Health (2 representatives)
Society of Community Medicine
Society of Education Officers
Welsh Joint Education Committee

Government department assessors

Department of Education and Science (3)
Department of Health and Social Security (3)
Northern Ireland, Ministry of Education (1)
Welsh Office (1)

Staff working for the NNEB

The day-to-day running of the Board is overseen by the Secretary to the Board. Professional staff consist of a Director of Courses and an Assistant Director of Courses, administrative officers and secretarial assistants.

To obtain a current list of colleges which run an NNEB course, send a stamped addressed envelope to:

National Nursery Examination Board
Argyle House
29–31 Euston Road
London NW1 2SD

NNEB courses

There are approximately 145 courses at present in England, Wales and Northern Ireland, and although they follow the same requirements for training and syllabus laid down by the Board, they are all different in some way or another, as each course interprets and develops according to local facilities and needs, and the opportunities that are available. For example, a course based in a rural setting may have good opportunities for the study of nature and, perhaps, outdoor pursuits. A course in a big city will have a large variety of interesting social settings for students to study and may afford easy access to museums. Whatever there is available each course tutor is at pains to use to the advantage of the students.

The pattern of attendance at college and practical placement for the equivalent of three and two days a week is arranged differently throughout the country. In some places students may find that they attend college for six days and then go to their practical placement for four. In others there may be block attendance at college for a month before going to practical placement or a week in, week out system may be used (see Table 3). These arrangements vary according to the college facilities and the practical placements available. The Board allows this flexibility in order to permit each college to arrange what is best for its area. The proportion of time spent at each place must, however, meet the Board's requirement of not less than seventy days in practical placement per year and not less than 105 days in college per year.

If for some reason you do not meet this requirement, your training will have to be extended to allow you to make up lost time. The Board allows a break in training of up to three months to be made up in this way. A longer break than this has to be referred to the Board for a decision about the length of training needed.

In the past many nursery nurses in training were given a small salary by the training authorities to which they were attached. These included local education authorities, departments of social services and voluntary bodies. Although there are still a few employer-based courses in some parts of the country, they are now a small minority. In 1977 80 per cent of colleges had only college-based students, 3 per cent had only employer-based students and the remaining colleges had a mixed employer/college intake.

	Sep 16	Sep 23	Sep 30	Oct 7	Oct 14	Oct 21	Oct 28	Nov 4	Nov 11	Nov 18	Nov 25	Dec 2	Dec 9	
Group A	1	1	1	0	1	0	1	0	1	0	1	0	1	8 weeks college / 5 weeks p.p.
Group B	1	1	0	1	0	1	1	1	0	1	0	1	0	8 weeks college / 5 weeks p.p.

(Induction — Group B, September)

	Jan 6	Jan 13	Jan 20	Jan 27	Feb 3	Feb 10	Feb 17	Feb 24	Mar 3	Mar 10	Mar 17	
Group A	1	0	1	1	1	0	1	0	1	0	1	7 weeks college / 4 weeks p.p.
Group B	0	1	1	1	0	1	0	1	0	1	0	6 weeks college / 5 weeks p.p.

	Apr 7	Apr 14	Apr 21	Apr 28	May 5	May 12	May 19	May 26	Jun 2	Jun 9	Jun 16	Jun 23	Jun 30	
Group A	0	1	0	1	0	1	0	Half-term	1	0	1	0	1	6 weeks college / 6 weeks p.p.
Group B	1	0	1	0	1	0	1	Holiday	0	1	0	1	1	7 weeks college / 5 weeks p.p.

p.p. = practical placement
1 = students in college
0 = students in practical placement

Totals:— Group A and B — 21 weeks college / 15 weeks practical placement / 36 week year

College-based courses run by local education authorities

Students are for the most part based in colleges of further education and technology. Full-time students are members of the college and go out to their practical placement as students. The primary responsibility for training belongs to the college and it is the tutors who would liaise with the staff in your practical placement about your experience during the time spent there.

Residential courses

Most colleges of further education do not provide residential accommodation. The local population attend on a daily basis. Some local authority courses do arrange lodgings for students when it is necessary because of transport difficulties.

Private nursery training colleges

There are four nursery training colleges which are residential and which normally charge fees. Students are not usually admitted to these colleges until they are 18 years of age and because of this, and the fact that the students have presumably continued their general education, they are allowed to take a shortened NNEB course lasting eighteen months. The same examination and certificate is awarded by the Board.

The residential nature of this training allows for considerable practical experience with babies and young children.

The names and addresses of these colleges will be included in the list you can obtain from the NNEB.

Grants and cost of courses

If you attend a college-based course at a local authority college, it is likely that you will pay no fees until you are over 18 years of age. In most cases this means that you are allowed to complete your two-year course free, even though you may be 18 just prior to completing it. The local authority may provide financial assistance for travelling, which might include, for instance, fares to college from home if you live more than three miles from

the college, and also fares from college to your practical placement. If such a grant is available your college may have special
forms for you to make such a claim. Some authorities give extra
help in the form of grants towards protective clothing, books
and stationery. The precise help given varies from one authority to another, and in addition discretionary grants are sometimes available to students under 18 years of age whose parents
are in financial difficulties. To obtain such grants, application
must be made to the local education authority.

Once you are 18 your local authority deals with any application for assistance to continue at a college course individually.

To find out about grants and costs at your local college
course, you should enquire at your local education authority.

*The interrelationship of theoretical and practical work and the importance
of each section of the training*

The NNEB training owes its success and popularity to the very
sensible interrelationship of theoretical and practical work
(figure 1).

You will read, discuss, listen and observe, and then you will
try out for yourself methods of caring for children. As you
practise, you will learn from the experienced staff whom you
work alongside, from your own reading, from your college
tutors and from your fellow students. By being given opportunities to try out for yourself different methods of working with
and caring for children, you will acquire skills which can
become really well developed from constant practice. Most
students will feel a natural response to children which will
assist immensely in the process, but experience is a tremendous
aid in knowing what's best, as any mother of three or four
children will tell you!

It is not uncommon for students to find they are more able in
one aspect of the training than the other. You may find the
theoretical side hard work, and therefore less attractive, or it
may be that you are shy and find working alongside adults in a
nursery very difficult, so that you are happy to retreat into a
book. But whichever may be the case, you must bear in mind
the importance of *both* parts of the training. It is no good
thinking that success in only one will suffice. A real effort must

be made to excel in all areas in which you work if you are going to achieve success as a trained nursery nurse.

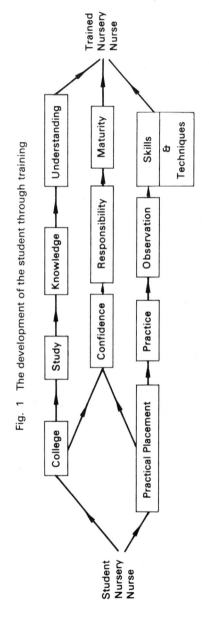

Fig. 1 The development of the student through training

Table 4. A College Timetable for an NNEB Course.

	MONDAY	TUESDAY	WEDNESDAY	THURSDAY	FRIDAY
MORNING	9.00 HEALTH 10.30 10.45 P.E. 12.00	9.00 ART 11.00 11.15 MUSIC 12.15	9.00 EARLY CHILD-HOOD EDUCATION 12.45	9.00 HEALTH - CHILD CARE PRACTICAL 12.00	9.00 CRAFT 10.30 10.45 MAN AND 12.15 HIS ENVIRON-MENT
AFTERNOON	1.00 TUTORIALS PRIVATE STUDY 3.00 SPOKEN ENGLISH	1.30 SOCIOLOGY 2.45 3.00 SOCIAL 4.30 POLICY	1.45 ELECTIVES 4.30	1.00 EDUCATION 3.15 3.30 ENGLISH 4.30	1.15 HOME ECONOMICS 4.30
EARLY EVENING			Some colleges may require students to attend classes in the evenings.		
EVENING					

You will soon see that your college work fits in well with your practical placement work. Tutors will talk about children's behaviour so that when you have to respond to a child, perhaps the very next day, you will act upon your new knowledge and adjust your response accordingly. Your environmental studies at college will prepare you to answer children's questions about plants, rocks and animals. These are only two examples, but in fact everything you do at college is planned to be of use and has real purpose in your training.

Methods of examination

To be entered for the NNEB examinations, candidates must show evidence of having completed an approved course of training. Form NNEB1, submitted by the college, states that the student has completed her training and applies for examination. In addition, Form NNEB2 furnishes a report on the student's work during the two years. Students must also submit to their course tutors records of observation of children made throughout the course. When these requirements are satisfactorily met, the candidate sits the written examination, which at the moment entails two papers lasting two and a half hours each.

Assessment

In order to provide information for Form 2 the college is involved in keeping a careful record of the student's progress both in college and in practical placement. This is a process of continuous assessment, and it means that everything you do right from the start of your course is considered as part of your training. In this system of training there is no opportunity for a student to be lazy and idle throughout the course and then pass easily on the written examination. Allowances are made for varying abilities and special skills, but great care is taken to ensure that no one becomes a qualified nursery nurse without first showing real ability and understanding of children and their needs.

To ensure a fair appraisal of the student's work, many different people are consulted by the course tutor, including practical placement staff and general studies tutors. Students are also encouraged to show off their own special abilities. Where one student may be musical, another may do beautiful needlework or tell stories particularly well. The course is designed to allow for individual growth as well as precise training in the skills you will later need. Above all, you must finally be able to show overall improvement and a satisfactorily high standard of ability in all aspects of the training.

Questions

1. How was the NNEB originally formed and how does it now operate?

2. How are the practical and theoretical parts of the NNEB course arranged and why is this procedure adopted?

3. Describe the method of assessment and examination which leads to the attainment of the NNEB Certificate.

III
College Studies

Further education

The 1944 Education Act defines further education as 'full-time and part-time education for persons over compulsory school age'. Full-time provision for senior pupils up to the age of 19 years of age is also provided in secondary education.

Further education includes all forms of education, in the widest sense, beyond the compulsory school age and is the third stage in education, the first and second being carried out in primary and secondary schools. The local education authority plays a leading role in the provision of further education, but voluntary groups (for example, the Workers' Education Association and the Women's Institute) also organise courses.

Further education courses take place in technical colleges, colleges of technology, colleges of further education, adult education centres and youth centres. These institutions, similar in function if not in name, offer a very large variety of full-time and part-time courses, both vocational and non-vocational, for the whole community from the age of 16. There is no upper age limit for students. The subjects studied range from preliminary stages to post-graduate level, and include courses for the professions, technical and craft training and recreation.

The NNEB course is one amongst many in such colleges. As a student you will enjoy meeting other students who are preparing for careers other than nursery nursing, as they will have a very wide variety of vocational and personal interests. This diversity of pursuits provides a very stimulating environment in which to work.

Although each college may have its own particular range and specialisation, depending on local demand, it is now common for most colleges to offer a wide choice of subjects. Every college has a freely available prospectus, which they will be pleased to send to you. Remember to mention whether you are interested in the full-time or part-time course prospectus when you enquire at your local college.

The following are only some examples of the courses which may be found in further education establishments, and will give you an idea of the various activities that take place in a college.

Technical and engineering courses

Engineering subjects might include mechanical engineering, electrical installation, welding and automobile engineering. Courses in mining engineering are offered in conjunction with National Coal Board training schemes. Building crafts are taught, including carpentry, brickwork, painting and decorating.

Training in hotel and catering technology includes courses in institutional management, catering, hotel reception, travel and tourism.

Science and maths are often allied to technical training schemes. Training is available, for example, for laboratory technicians.

Professional and vocational courses

Courses are run in social and administrative studies. Business studies includes a number of subjects such as economics, computer science, statistics, law and accounts. Secretarial training is offered, ranging from basic typing courses to bi-lingual secretarial courses with foreign language shorthand and postgraduate secretarial and administrative studies.

Some of the courses offered have particular professional goals in view. A physical education course, offered alongside GCE 'A' level studies, prepares candidates for application to colleges of education which specialise in training teachers of physical education. Courses in agriculture offer farm management, agricultural mechanics, and horticulture.

Vocational courses include hairdressing and beauty culture, home economics and dressmaking.

Schools of art, music and drama

Art departments offer a wide range of courses. There is a full-time, two-year foundation course in art and design, which is a preliminary for students wishing to go on to professional training. In addition, there are courses in jewellery making, fine art, ceramics, photography, sculpture and fashion. Although all of these are available on a full-time basis, they are also popular part-time subjects for leisure pursuits.

Studies in music and drama can also be pursued and are sometimes combined with technical training to prepare for work in the theatre, radio or television.

Languages

A full range of courses in foreign languages is offered and they are particularly popular as both day and evening part-time courses. Such courses not only provide opportunities for the public to learn a language for their own private interests and use on holiday, but also serve the needs of businessmen whose work takes them abroad. English is also taught as a foreign language to immigrants and visitors to this country.

General education and examinations

Many subjects are also offered in colleges in the form of GCE syllabuses at both 'O' and 'A' level. It is sometimes possible for students to take a subject in GCE at the same time as a vocational course. The General Certificate of Education is offered by a number of different regional examining bodies.

Examinations offered in the colleges lead to certificates and diplomas of qualification, which are suitable either for employment purposes or for entry to more advanced further training.

The need for qualifications in a wide range of special subjects has led to examinations being offered by a diverse number of examining bodies. These include the following: City and Guilds of London Institute, Royal Society of Arts, London Chamber of Commerce, Institute of Linguistics, Central Council for Education and Training, Union of Educational Institutes and National Nursery Examination Board.

College programmes and organisation

As can be seen from the previous section, the variety of courses in a college of further education is enormous. This is one of its main strengths and attractions. Such a college provides a glimpse of a cross-section of the working lives of our society.

As a student you are not only able to pursue your own particular interests and training, but also to widen your knowledge of how people in other sections of society are trained and organised.

Liberal or elective studies and college activities

It is not uncommon for colleges to put aside one afternoon a week when all full-time students are combined in a glorious mix of interesting pursuits, sometimes called 'liberal' or 'elective' studies. Almost any subject or activity can be on the programme, students often making their own suggestions for activities they wish to pursue. They can include any of the subjects mentioned previously, so that if, for example, a hairdresser wishes to make jewellery, this might be the time she will choose 'to do it. Outdoor pursuits and indoor hobbies are popular, and the following are some of the activities that might be included: sailing, football, hockey, swimming, badminton, table tennis, gymnastics, dancing, painting, pottery, sculpture, chess, bridge, cookery, foreign languages, typing, music, choir, instrumental groups, community service, woodwork, metalwork, car maintenance, first aid, macramé.

Apart from this ideal opportunity to pursue personal interests, you are given an excellent chance to meet and spend time with the students from other courses. Your social development as a student is catered for in this way, as well as your intellectual development. The social life in a college is of great benefit to you and is the first step into the adult world. You may wish to join the students' organisations at college, and much is to be gained from participation in extra curricular activities such as camping or field study trips, fund raising efforts for charities or political activities.

College facilities

The technical and vocational subjects studied in colleges need particular facilities and accommodation. Engineering workshops are equipped with machinery and tools; catering departments have real catering kitchens for students to use. Science subjects require laboratories; horticulture demands glasshouses. Hairdressing is taught in especially equipped salons which mirror the work situation to be found in real life. As well as these specialised facilities, there is very comprehensive provision for study in all subject areas. The art school has large and small studios; the secretarial courses are equipped with typwriters and business machines; craft rooms have very large tables, and so on. A music room will be sound-proofed or separate from the main building and will have small separate practice rooms as well as all kinds of musical instruments and recording equipment. Language laboratories will provide modern audio systems for teaching and learning languages.

It is usual for each course to have its own room as a base. In addition there are communal facilities, such as a sports hall, refectory, students' common room, library and audio-visual resource rooms where students can study and use audio-visual aids. There is usually a large lecture hall, as well as small class rooms, which are used for different types of lectures. Occasionally a visiting speaker may be invited to address a large number of students.

The NNEB course also has special provision. There is usually a 'base' room for the NNEB students, which may be furnished to meet all the different requirements of the vocational element of the course, i.e. lectures, discussions, group seminar, tutorials and practical workshops. There may be a sectioned-off, comfortable area for sitting for group discussion. The room usually has adequate display area, a class library, a good selection of children's books and a sink with hot and cold water. There is often a separate health room, which is furnished to provide especially for that area of the syllabus which covers the practical care of infants.

It is often the case that the course tutor has an office which doubles as a tutorial room where students can be seen privately to discuss their work and progress.

The NNEB syllabus

The NNEB has drawn up a systematically thought-out syllabus to suit the needs of young people in training. A careful balance of vocational and general studies has been planned, so that you not only learn all about young children but also develop through further education at your own level.

The syllabus (appendix A) gives guidance to colleges on areas of study which should be covered but does not lay down an exact curriculum, and this enables colleges to interpret the syllabus and develop an individual programme within it. The course then fits local needs and suits the students involved. College study time is divided into approximately half vocational and half general studies. You should not make the mistake of thinking that only your vocational studies are really important, as every part of both the college studies and the practical training are relevant.

Vocational studies

The vocational studies are planned to supplement your work with the children in practical placement, so that practical training has a sound base of theory on which to proceed. The studies can be broken down into three main areas, although they, too, interrelate with each other.

1. The family and society (figure 2)

The young child cannot be considered in isolation, as he is part of a family which is in turn part of our society. A study of family life, its changing patterns and parental responsibility as society sees it, provides a background to the study of young children.

The ethical and spiritual values we offer to young children must be considered. Cultural patterns differ according to locality, national origins and class. The differing living conditions in which children find themselves must be studied; housing difficulties such as high-rise flats and overcrowding must be considered. How does the child living in the country fare, com-

pared with the child living in the inner city? You will learn about local provision for education and about the health and social services. The introduction to school life, for both the child and the parent, has to be seen as part of the community service which professionally qualified people provide. The work of these different professions and their function in the community are studied.

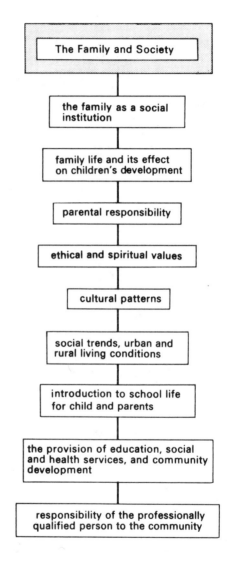

Fig. 2 Vocational Studies

2. Child development and child care (figure 3)

Your observations of children form the core of a study of child development and child care. Human development and the developmental stages of the child from birth to 7 years are studied; consideration is given to the physical, intellectual, emotional and social development of young children. These studies form a base for the understanding of the various needs of young children and how best to provide for them which is the main goal of a qualified nursery nurse.

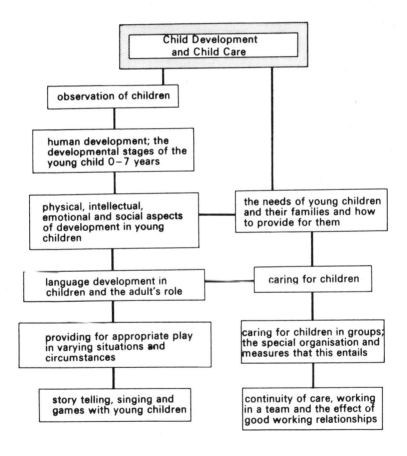

Fig. 3 Vocational Studies

Special attention is paid to a study of language development and the part adults play in assisting children to develop their speech and understanding. The importance of play is seen in the light of the study of development, and you learn how to provide for different types of play in many varying situations.

You will learn how to tell stories and how to participate with children in activities such as music, games and rhymes. The fact that the nursery nurse may be working with children in groups is remembered, since different types of care may be necessary as a result. The nursery nurse must be aware of the need for continuity of care and the importance of working well in a team. In such circumstances good working relationships will result in a happy atmosphere for children to grow in.

3. The health of the young child (figure 4)

This part of the syllabus includes every aspect of caring for the health of children. The promotion of good health for all, through correct nutrition, exercise and rest, is studied. You learn how to prevent and control the spread of infection, how to prevent accidents and how to administer elementary first aid. The programme also includes the care of the unwell or convalescent child and, finally, personal hygiene, which nursery nurses practise and teach to children. The practical baby care sessions are usually included in this section of the syllabus.

Practical workshop

The NNEB course usually includes practical work which assists you in your training. A practical workshop session is often included, when you make things which will be useful to you in your work with children. This might include storytelling aids, scrapbooks, percussion instruments, dressing-up clothes, toys, play food, etc. All of these activities tie in with the syllabus section on 'provision for play'. There is usually also practical work in the care of babies. You may practise on baby-weight dolls and learn such things as how to bath, change and feed infants, before you try to do these things with a real baby.

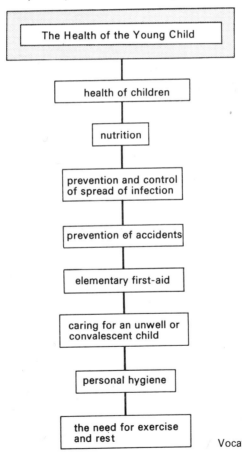

Fig. 4
Vocational Studies

General studies

You must never be tempted to underestimate the importance of
the general studies element of the course. The NNEB syllabus
states: 'Children need the companionship of lively minds and it
is hoped that students will take every opportunity to enrich
their own interests.' Combined with the college activities and
life as a student, the general studies subjects provide a really
well-rounded education for the school leaver. But you will find
that the general studies subjects will also prove useful in relation to the vocational studies and will often help you in your
work with children. These subjects, too, are divided into three
main areas.

1.   Home and society (figure 5)

This section of the syllabus will include a study of sociology.
Such questions as individual rights and responsibilities,
attitudes to social problems and the pressures on society will be
considered. Study of human behaviour, relationships, religions

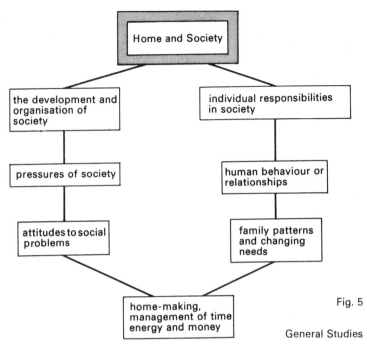

Fig. 5

General Studies

and changing family patterns will extend your own education and understanding and will also enable you to understand more fully how best to care for children. Home-making studies and consideration of the consumer and the best use of time and money will stand you in good stead no matter where you work and live as an adult. Often colleges also include cookery, dressmaking or needlework in this section of the syllabus.

2. Communication and the creative arts (figure 6)

The ability to communicate well is an important skill in all human beings. To communicate well verbally is an essential requirement for a nursery nurse. All of the training entails the use of spoken language, and you may find you are able to take Spoken English as a subject. Written English and the study of literature, poetry and drama extend this ability to communicate, as do studies in the creative arts. These might include painting, pottery, sculpture, craft, music and movement.

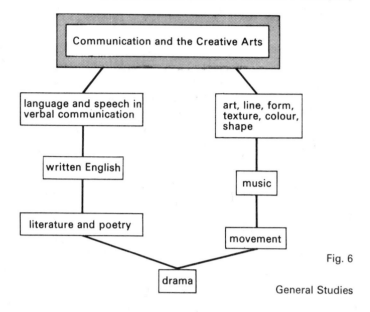

Fig. 6

General Studies

You will grow in confidence as you acquire the ability to express yourself fully. You will also mature emotionally and socially through an understanding of and familiarity with your own developing abilities in the creative arts. This ability will also help you in your work with children when you tell them stories and enjoy music and art activities together.

3. Man and his environment (figure 7)

This area of study aims to give you knowledge of how man is placed in his surroundings. This subject will include a study of living things, the variety of life forms, their interdependence, pollution, modern trends and pressures on the environment. You may find you are able to participate in field studies or outdoor pursuits under this section of the syllabus.

General studies are sometimes approached in a thematic way, so that as a student you might work for a short time on a project (say a dramatic entertainment for children) in the production of which the English, drama, music, movement and art tutors all assist you and your fellow students.

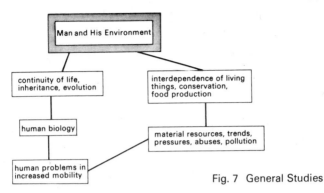

Fig. 7 General Studies

Each college will have its own method of timetabling. Some colleges arrange for students to study a subject for a short, intensive period; others plan for a subject to be studied for the whole of the two-year course. Some colleges block the vocational and general studies separately; others integrate them. As you can see, the vocational and general studies subjects of the NNEB course interact well and provide a very suitable framework for your work as a nursery nurse (see figure 8).

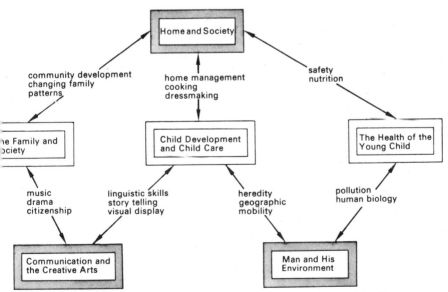

Fig. 8 Vocational and General Studies

Study skills

The many different facets of the NNEB training make it imperative that you go about your studies in an organised and methodical way. Whatever pattern of practical placement is used, it should be possible to establish a regular routine, in which time for study is set aside each week.

College tutors will guide you about what work needs to be done. Only by keeping up with the work will you be able to make the best of all the training offered. You will need to assume a great deal of responsibility for your own work and study, which will be somewhat different from the school experience that you have just left behind you.

Every college will approach the question of students' work differently, but with the demands of the NNEB syllabus it is safe to assume that you will be expected to produce written work regularly. Each term you will need to write up notes, write essays, write up observations of children and write answers to set questions. In addition, you may be asked to prepare a special topic in project form. All of this work will be set against a background of reading, lectures, discussions and tutorials, for which the taking of notes will be necessary.

Where to study

Try to find a suitable place to study which is a regular working spot, so that you form the habit of studying there. When choosing a place to study the following points need to be considered. You will need a table and a chair to sit up in. Avoid sitting in a lounging chair. The room should be well lit and at the right temperature. Too warm, and you will feel sleepy; too cold, and you will be distracted. There should be good ventilation. Avoid distractions such as the noise of people talking or a radio. There should be no interruptions while you are working.

It may be that a library will suit you. You may at times need to work in a library anyway to consult reference books for your work. If you work at home, arrange your room so that you will be able to study comfortably. Explain to the family that you should not be disturbed and tell friends which evenings you will be studying so that you are not interrupted.

Libraries and books

As soon as you start college you should make yourself familiar with the library and with the class reference books available to you. Learn to use the catalogue, and find out how many books you can borrow and for how long. What journals are available to you and where are they kept? Do the tutors provide reading lists, and are you expected to buy some books for yourself? When using a book try first to get an idea of its contents by looking through, checking the contents list, and seeing who wrote it and for what purpose. The date of publication will tell you if it is up to date. Is there an index or some relevant appendixes? Develop the practice of skimming through books in order to find the information relevant to you at that moment. After this reading should be done more thoroughly but try to read quickly. It is better to read a chapter through quickly three times than very slowly once. You will absorb and understand the content more easily in this way. Avoid sitting for half an hour with the same page open in front of you, struggling to digest the meaning of the words. If set reading should prove very difficult, discuss this with your tutor as you will receive help. If you have a dictionary always at hand, you can look up specific words that you do not understand and this will help not only in your reading but in increasing your vocabulary.

Note taking

It helps to keep a record of your reading in note form. Write the title and name of the author of each book as well as the publisher. Brief notes on the contents, with main headings underlined and a summary of what each section is about, will prove useful to you both in revision and to refer to when you are writing essays. Space out these notes well so that you can find what you want easily. Read the chapter through first before you start making notes and make sure that the book is one which is recommended by your tutor.

Taking notes from a book or lecture forces you to concentrate and is, therefore, a useful practice. Even if you do not use the notes again, you will still remember more if you write down something as you go along. If you take clear notes, however, they will be most helpful to you in your future studies. Look for key points. Number the points as you go and set them out in a pattern so that they are easy to see and remember.

Using your own words to record what is said in a lecture or in a television or radio programme will help you to understand and remember what you hear. You will not be able to write down everything. Brief but concise notes are what you must aim to achieve.

Learning and memorising facts

There will be times when you will need to remember facts in order to reproduce them for examination. There are a number of techniques you can use to help you.

1. Taking the first letter of each word to form another word can help. For example: 'A child's *n*eeds are *i*ntellectual, *p*hysical, *e*motional, and *s*ocial gives you NIPES.

2. Remember the facts in a visual form. This should be easy if you associate them with your observations of children. In remembering a specific play situation you should be able to list the preparation, the materials used, how they are used, the values to the children and the completion of the activity. This orderly procedure should assist your memory so that you leave nothing out.

3. Write lists of facts on a piece of paper that you carry around with you. Look at it often and each time it will become more familiar.

Essays

Essay writing serves a number of purposes. Having to express your ideas in writing will clarify your thoughts about a particular topic. If you have not understood a point, your tutor will see this and explain your error to you. By writing the essay you have to demonstrate that you understand clearly what you have learned.

It is important to ensure before you start that you understand the question. Look at it carefully. Are there two or three parts to the question? If so, answer each section separately, with sub-headings underlined. Look for key words in the question which will help you to see what is required in the answer. You may be asked to 'describe', 'discuss', 'compare', 'contrast', 'define'. A methodical approach to essay writing is essential. Plan all the points you want to make, first jotting everything down roughly. Then group the points into sections which seem relevant.

Take this question as an example: *Children enjoy playing with sand. How can a nursery nurse ensure that this is a purposeful experience for children in a nursery?*

This question might best be answered in four separate sections:

1. describe sand play provision (i.e. equipment) and when and how it is provided;
2. describe how children play with it (examples from your own observations might illustrate this);
3. state what the children learn in this type of play (experimentation, volume, social development, language, etc.);
4. state what the nursery nurse's part should be in both providing and extending the play.

Make sure that your written work follows an orderly pattern. Start with an introduction and end with a concluding paragraph.

Projects

Collecting and presenting information in a project can be a very enjoyable learning activity. Take care to balance the project with a fair amount of your own written comment and examples which form illustrative material for the text.

To conclude, as a college student you should be prepared to take advantage of every kind of learning opportunity which is offered to you. Listen to radio programmes, read a daily newspaper and approach each day with an enquiring and alert mind, and you will find that your student days at college will prove to be really worth while.

Questions

1. Describe the range of courses available in a college of further education. What is the best way to learn about them?

2. What subjects are studied on the NNEB course which could be called 'vocational'?

3. Why are the general studies subjects in the NNEB syllabus as important as the vocational studies? What do they include?

4. How can a student meet a wide variety of other students and enter fully into the life of the college she attends?

5. Why is it important to develop a study routine? How can a student make sure that time spent studying is useful and productive?

IV

The Student in Practical Placement

Working alongside a team of adults and the people you will meet

The practical experience you gain during your training is a vital part of the course. It is often the part of the training most attractive to students who want to get on with actually working with children. It is a great opportunity for you and you must make the most of this valuable time.

Practical placements are chosen carefully and basic experience gained by students must be with normal children. Students with a special interest will possibly be able to visit particular establishments, for example where handicapped children are cared for. Tutors do try to place students in practical placements which are convenient for travelling and provide the experience most suited to each individual.

An important part of your experience in practical placement will be your adjustment to working in a team. Since you will be a student, you will be the most junior member of that team, but for all that you can play an essential part in the smooth running of the organisation.

It will be necessary for you to familiarise yourself with the hierarchy, that is, who is in charge of what and over whom. You may find that everyone feels he or she should tell you what to do as you are so much in need of direction, but this could lead to your being asked to do two different things at the same time! In order to avoid this, be prepared to clear such difficulties up cheerfully and politely, so that you offend no one and hurt no one's feelings. Try to find out early on which member of staff is particularly concerned with your training and discuss matters with him or her as frankly as you can.

A student can easily upset the balance in a team working situation. The qualified staff might sometimes feel it is easier to do things themselves than suffer the ineptitude of a student trying to learn new skills. Think how much easier it is for us to dress a three-year-old ourselves rather than allow him to learn by slowly trying to dress himself, and you will understand the type of feeling that the staff may have.

There is a great difference between a student nursery nurse and a qualified nursery nurse, as you will soon see by the amount of responsibility that is assumed by the qualified nursery nurses you work with.

The role of the qualified nursery nurse differs according to the place in which she works. Her training and qualification fit her to care for the whole child in any given situation. This care includes supervision and assistance in the physical, mental, emotional and social development of the child. When a nursery nurse works alongside other professionals, it is important that she understands her role and how it differs from theirs. As a student you must notice and learn these differences.

When you work with a teacher, you should know that the teacher has been trained particularly in the education of young children. She has studied in great depth the mental development of children and has specific skills and training in helping them to develop successfully. A teacher is, of course, well aware that you cannot separate the mental development of the child from his physical, emotional and social development and is concerned that all these needs are being met. But her special training fits her to assist children in the learning process, to offer them the structure on which to build themselves up. The teacher may direct the nursery nurse to assist with some of these processes and will wish to discuss with her the progress of the children.

The nursery nurse also differs from a nurse. The medical nurse has training in medicine and health and knows a great deal about ill health and how to care for people who are ill. Her experience and training will have included practical work with new-born babies, but it is possible she will have had little experience with normal healthy children and how to provide for their all-round needs. If you are working with a nurse in a hospital, she will be in a position to understand better the medical needs of the particular children. The sister in charge will direct you in your work, in order that the special skills of nursery nursing should be put to use.

The social worker is also different from the nursery nurse. Social workers are usually graduates and have trained professionally to help people in all walks of life. They usually help people in difficulties, which can range from a family with one member in prison to an old person unable to cope with living alone. In their work with families they will, of course, be concerned for the children as well as the adults. If you work with a social worker, you will see that he or she is concerned with a wider area of social problems than a nursery nurse may be when she works with a socially disadvantaged child.

The nursery nurse may also work with playgroup leaders and voluntary workers. These people may have professional qualifications or they may have only personal experience to go on when working with children. Their own experience may be extremely valuable and affects greatly how much they are able to offer the children.

The nursery nurse course includes a small part of each of the above professional trainings. Nursery nurse students are taught by qualified teachers, qualified nurses who are health visitors and qualified social workers. This training is the only one which includes all aspects of the care of young children in one course, and makes the trained nursery nurse adaptable to work in any situation with children from birth to 7 years.

Recognition of the special skills and ability of each member of the team in any working relationship is very important to the success of such co-operation and the happiness not only of those working together but also of the children concerned.

You will notice different atmospheres whenever you go into a building where people work together. A friendly, happy place reflects good working relationships and is often the result of a few people who seem to live their lives in such a way. Equally, an unhappy person can affect others and all those working around her.

In addition to professionals that you will meet, you will also meet support service workers such as cooks, cleaners, caretakers and delivery men. These people are just as essential to the smooth and happy running of an establishment as the person in charge. Cheerfulness and good manners from a student will be her contribution to the happy atmosphere.

It is not unusual for students to be going through difficult developmental stages themselves and it sometimes occurs that some personal upset may be making the student feel very unhappy. If this happens, it can easily have an affect on the student's work and on the people she is with all day, particularly when she is in quite a small organisation with close working conditions. The mature people you are working with are usually sympathetic to such difficulties and 'growing pains', but this sympathy should not be exploited, as patience may eventually wear thin if you are a constant worry. Make an effort, therefore, to leave your own worries behind you as you step into your work. This ability is an essential professional quality which we all have to strive to attain, no matter how difficult our lives seem to be at times, and the temptation to indulge ourselves in our misery is one of the things we have to try to overcome as mature adults.

One of the things which annoys staff concerned with students is a seeming lack of concern for detail. It will, of course, take a student longer to do chores at the very start of her training, but staff will be irritated if the job you have been given has to be gone over again by them. Try to leave things tidy and in their place. Find out which containers are used for paste rather than helping yourself to a jam jar which may be needed for something else. Staff will have an agreed routine which makes their work easier and smooth running. By finding out and fitting in with this routine as quickly as you can, you will avoid upsets and disruption and will learn much more quickly.

Establishments vary a great deal in this matter of routines and duties, but you will find that efficient organisation leaves the most time for the staff to talk and play with the children. If you understand this, you will see the importance of doing your set duties efficiently.

One of the difficult things a student needs to judge correctly is the amount of initiative she shows. This means that she must gauge carefully what she does without being told because she thinks it needs doing. The set routines and methods established in a group of staff usually ensure that each member of that team knows his or her role. It is likely that there will be a rota of duties for the staff, which involves them in different duties each day. One of these might be bathroom duty, for instance, which might include supervision of the children when they go to the toilet and wash, and mopping up spills afterwards so that the bathroom is left clean and tidy. There will be other duties, such as helping the children to set tables for dinner, cleaning babies' bibs after meals and supervising various play areas both indoors and out. The routine will be planned so that staff share all these jobs and each has a turn at different duties. (You will see that if one member of staff decides she wants to go into the book corner and read to the children for half an hour, she will have to consider first whether she is expected to be somewhere else; otherwise there could be an area in which the children are left unsupervised.)

There will be other agreed procedures. You may find that the staff agree that whoever first sees something spilled or is nearest to the mess wipes it up; that the person who discovers a child with wet clothing changes him; that there are agreed arrangements for the administration of first aid; that there are rules about who answers the phone. Since all these events take a member of staff away from his or her normal duties, another member of staff has to be aware of this and must be ready to help.

It is not altogether surprising, therefore, that one hears comments about students showing 'not enough' or 'too much' initiative. Being aware of your working situation and sensitive to the needs and feelings of all those around you will enable you to apply yourself correctly in a constantly changing situation. For one thing which you will find in your training is that you will be expected to become an adaptable person who can apply your knowledge and skills in any situation where you are working with children.

You will be placed for your practical work in an establishment where the example of caring for children which you will see has been considered suitable for training new nursery nurses. The facilities and provision will be good, and the staff you work alongside will be qualified and therefore able to train you. They will be fully occupied with their normal jobs (any

routine which involves looking after children is a very demanding one). Remember this and you will appreciate the time they
find to talk to you and to help you. Remember, also, that you
are not the first or the only student who will have passed
through the practical placement. Staff take on young, inexperienced students each year; by the end of the year, when the
student has learned a great deal and has got to know the staff
and routines of the establishment, it will be time for her to move
on and the staff will be faced with yet another new inexperienced student. Staff normally carry on this extra duty of training cheerfully and enthusiastically, but it is not surprising that
they may become impatient if a student seems uncaring or
casual. Once you have become qualified it is likely that you will
find yourself training students. It is worth keeping these points
in mind as you start at a new practical placement.

Professional attitudes and confidential information

One of the first things you will be told, both at college and in
practical placement, is that information you hear about children through your work must not be discussed with others not
specifically involved in your work. Of course, you will go home
brimming over with things to talk about, but try to develop a
method of discussing things generally without mentioning
specific children or cases. Ask yourself to answer truthfully, do
I like to gossip? We all have a tendency to do this and it is
something to be watched. The next time you are about to pass
on a bit of information you've heard about someone, ask yourself if it is important that the next person should know about it,
and if the information is in any way malicious or unkind. If it is,
resolve to stop being a gossip and talk about something else.

One reason that you should use discretion about what you
hear at practical placement should be very clear. You may hear
information of a confidential nature; for example, that a child
has only one parent, that he has a disability, that he is adopted,
etc. The list of things is endless, and it is obviously in your
power to repeat these things outside. 'Power' is a good word to
think about, too. Doesn't it make us feel important that we
know something confidential? It's a real temptation to pass on

information in order to demonstrate our own importance to another person.

But if you value your own opinion of yourself, the trust which has been put in your integrity by the college staff in selecting you for training and by the practical placement staff in welcoming you into their establishment, then you will find no difficulty in adopting a professional and mature attitude towards the people and children with whom you come into contact.

If you should find yourself in a practical placement for training which is near to your home, you may find yourself in particular difficulty over information about children. People you know will ask you about the children. How are they doing? What happened between those two boys yesterday? etc. It will be necessary for you to employ a great deal of tact and care in your answers. An unguarded statement such as 'That Tommy's a real little devil at school' might have very serious repercussions, even though you could well have said this light-heartedly and with fondness. The fact that you are now seen as part of that school gives much more importance to your words than if you were speaking as a private person, and it could be that you are labelling a child quite unjustly and doing a great harm to both him and his parents.

Similarly, I have heard of conversations between students on buses being overheard and commented upon. If you do find that because you live locally this is a real problem for you, discuss the difficulties with the staff at practical placement and your course tutor. They will help you to be prepared with the right answers. A good tip if you are asked about a child you are helping with, is to think of something you have recently seen him doing and to tell the parent about it. You might say that he 'played with Johnny at brick building for a long time yesterday' or that a little girl 'loves dressing up'. These factual comments will demonstrate that you know the child and that you are interested in what he does. That you are not prepared to discuss wider implications of the child's activities will be demonstrated. If you are pressed further on such points, it is wise to refer the parent to a member of staff. You can, if necessary, point out that you are a student.

It is interesting to note that some parents may feel more able to talk to you as a student than to a member of the staff. This

will be especially so with a parent who is lacking in confidence
and sees the staff as representing authority and perhaps a
threat. It is very important that you tactfully encourage parents
to talk to a member of staff. If you receive information from a
parent, it would usually be wise to pass on the information to
the member of staff in charge, but you may, of course, consider
the information confidential. If it does not have any bearing at
all on the care of the child in the practical placement then you
may be right not to repeat it.

Some students feel uncomfortable about being 'only a student' in practical placement. Remember that this is a tempor-
ary state of affairs and that it has very great advantages, even
though, if you have a great deal of confidence, you may well feel
you could take over the role of a full member of staff. As a
student you are not responsible for overall organisation and
supervision and this is a good thing because it enables you to try
out various things without the worry of such overall responsibility. It gives you time — which is so valuable — to think about
what you do with the children, and to observe how they react in
different situations, learning as you go.

I have found that students are uncommonly interested in the
abnormal and are eager to plunge in with sweeping comments
about children, applying labels with gay abandon. This is quite
an understandable development, as students' interest and
reading widens their understanding of the whole complex picture of childhood as it begins to emerge. I would advise caution
in jumping to conclusions. You will find that highly qualified
professionals are very careful in choosing their words to
describe a child. They appreciate the infinite variety of human
development and behaviour and try always to approach children with the most positive expectations in mind. They have
also learned from experience that quick comments and conclusions about a child can so very often be proved wrong and can
be harmful. Remember, too, that only one side of a child may be
seen when he is away from his home. As a student you will, of
course, have opinions about what you see. They may be accurate or quite misguided, and it will be very good for you to
discuss your ideas with the staff at practical placement, with
other students and with college tutors. One of the difficult
things about child rearing is that each child needs to be treated

differently. We can decide on basic principles as guidelines from our knowledge of what children need as they grow and develop. We do, however, have to be adaptable. This is one of the things which makes it so interesting. What is right for one child may be quite wrong for another and it is only by experience, study and thought that you will develop the knowledge to make the best decision of how to treat each child. Sensitivity and respect of others' feelings will be a very useful quality in guiding your decisions. You may be surprised at the action you see another adult take with a child, but remember that you may not know all the facts.

As a student you must be prepared to question and reason so that you have a basis for your own future actions. Take care not to offend the staff you are working with by the manner in which you question. Your questions should be put in an enquiring way and not be thrown out as a challenge. Qualified staff have feelings and pride in their work, just as you will when you complete your training. Give them the respect they deserve and you will find they respond to you with help and kindness.

Creating a good first impression

You will have made a great effort to be accepted on an NNEB course and so undoubtedly you will approach your first practical placement with pleasure and perhaps some nervousness. Some of us find 'first days' exciting and thrilling, but there are also those of us who may be overcome with fear and dread. Let me reassure the latter that they will have a lot of support from all the people they meet and that the staff in practical placement *do* welcome students. Otherwise you would not have been sent. But there are a few things which you can do which will ease you through the first few weeks.

Dress

You may be tempted to dress smartly, which is quite normal on your first day. But your best clothes are unlikely to be suitable for working with children, so think carefully about this. Being on your feet all day will be a change from your normal experience at school when you sat down a good deal. Stacked shoes and slip-on sandals are not suitable — they might even be unsafe. The important thing is that you must be comfortable and that you can move easily and quickly when necessary. Students often feel most comfortable in jeans and they may be suitable for work but this depends very much on where you work and how the staff there feel. They would not be a good choice for a first morning, and if they are ever worn should be clean and neat rather than tatty as may be the fashion! Avoid wearing expensive sheer tights as they won't last long. You may need an overall, perhaps two. One might be a 'clean' overall, for cooking or working with babies. It will serve the purpose of protecting the baby from your normal clothes and so must always be immaculately clean. The other overall might be for 'dirty' work, e.g. mixing paint and clay, etc. If you have long hair, tie it back so that it doesn't hang in the children's faces when you lean over them. In short, you must be neat and tidy so that you look as if you are ready for working with children.

Staffroom manners

Most establishments welcome students into their staffroom and, except in a few circumstances where overcrowding is a problem, you will probably have social contact with staff there. It is difficult to change from a schoolgirl into an adult in under two months but this, in fact, is what you have to do. Establishing friendly relationships with the adults you work with is not an easy task to an inexperienced young person. There is always the danger of being too familiar (remember you are a student and quite a bit younger than the rest of the staff), or more often students are too shy and say nothing at all, which makes contact difficult. Try to be friendly and cheerful and respond to the staff as well as you can. Take care not to sit in a comfortable chair when staff are coming in and there is nowhere for them to sit. Make sure you help others to drinks, sugar, etc. It is often the case that a student finds a motherly friend in the cook and happily confides in her about all her weekend activities, but some caution in this might be wise. It is possible that what you say may be passed on to the rest of the staff and, before you know it, your Saturday night activities might be cause for general concern. Generally speaking, your personal life should be kept for out-of-work time except, of course, for light conversation.

Timekeeping and absence

Naturally, you must arrive at your practical placement in good time to start the day. You should also try to arrange to leave when the rest of the staff leave. A poor impression will be given if you always rush off early to catch a bus, but it may be impossible to avoid this. If this is so, try to find some way of making up the time. Could you take some job home to do in the evening, for example?

If you have to be absent when you are expected at your practical placement, you must make sure to let them know and explain your absence. Try to avoid any unnecessary absences by making dental appointments, etc.; at other times. Your college will give you instructions about all these procedures.

Making a contribution to the establishment in which you train

Although you are a student, it is most likely that you will be welcomed into your practical placement and made to feel part of the establishment. This welcome should result in a response from you which includes involvement and a general concern for what is going on. You should feel you want to contribute something as well as learning, which is mainly for your own benefit. Be alert, therefore, to ways in which you can contribute. If the practical placement needs egg boxes, help by bringing them. If you have a special talent, such as playing a musical instrument, persevere with it despite your shyness and lack of confidence, so that you can bring your instrument for the children to see and hear. Look at your own possessions. Is there something special that children would find interesting that you could take to practical placement to show them and talk about? Children appreciate such things and also your efforts on their behalf, and the staff will be pleased to see evidence of your interest.

If you are good with your hands, you will find plenty of opportunities to make things to be used in your practical placement. You may find that you are given help in this at college, in craft or needlework classes. Some colleges make this an intrinsic part of the course and assess the work just as other aspects of training are assessed. This is, again, an area of your work which you will be advised about by your course tutor.

If the practical placement has an evening function, try to make every effort to attend. There may be fund raising events when your help will be appreciated, or social events for parents and friends where your attendance will be noted with pleasure.

Routine duties in your first term

One of the good things about being a completely new student in your first year is that you cannot be expected to know anything about the practical placement. At first people will expect to have to tell you what to do and where things are. Take advantage of this time and ask questions so that you understand what is required of you. If you don't, and are still unsure of what you should be doing a few months later, then of course people will be less ready to spend time explaining things to you. The ability to see what needs to be done and when it is appropriate for you to do it is a very individual procedure which comes more easily to some than to others. How much you should do without direction also depends very much upon the establishment in which you are working and the preferences of the staff who are training you. This will differ greatly from one establishment to another but wherever you are watch how the staff do things and you will soon learn the routines.

Your approach to children

Until you started college you could yourself have been called a child, and you have now to take on the role of an adult when dealing with children. This is rather different from being an older child who plays with young children. You may be tempted to pick up and cuddle them and join in with rough-and-tumble play. Although there is nothing wrong with these activities, they may be unsuitable in the situation in which you are placed as a student. Dealing with children in groups, for instance, will call for a different approach from dealing with one or two children. Of course, the type of approach you take will vary greatly with the age of the children. We are finding out more and more about the great value of individual adult attention to young children, so what you say and do with the children is extremely important. It will be best to take your cue from the qualified staff you are working with. You will soon see how and why they work with children in the way they do, and you can learn a great deal by watching and listening.

The way the nursery nurse student fits in during her training

The nursery school

A number of the nursery schools now used for training have a long history of training nursery nurses. Their staffing includes teachers and qualified nursery assistants and they are, therefore, well aware of the needs of the student nursery nurse. A student is usually placed with a teacher who has special responsibility for her, and the nursery assistant who works with that teacher will also take part in advising the student. It is the head teacher of the establishment who has overall responsibility for the student whilst in practical placement and she will want to see the student regularly to discuss work and the written observations of children which are undertaken at the school.

The staff will start by letting you settle into the routine gradually and will then give you more and more of the specific tasks at school to do in order that you can learn them all. You will be given breaks, as all the staff are, and the routine will be arranged with your presence in mind, so that your unexpected absence will cause some necessary adjustments. Students in training are now always supernumerary (that is, in excess of the number of staff who would normally be provided in an establishment). This means that students can be allowed time to learn the work without the pressure that was previously involved when students were counted as part of the staffing allowance.

The students need to try out various projects and this has to be arranged by the class teacher and nursery assistant. They will usually allow a student to plan a particular activity each week and take a story and music session. If the teacher has two

students who alternate she sometimes feels that her own programme for the children is disrupted and that she and the
nursery assistant do not have sufficient time to themselves with
the children. It is worth thinking about this aspect so that you
will understand better how they feel.

Nursery schools keep normal school hours and as a student
you will be expected to keep the same hours as the staff, which
means arriving in good time to prepare for the children and
staying at the end to clear up. More and more nursery schools
now have children for half the day, so that the programme is
repeated in the morning and afternoon. This is a demanding
routine, as it means there are fresh children in the afternoon all
eager to start when you may be beginning to tire. There are
usually also some children who stay all day and they have to be
provided for during the lunch period. You will soon see that the
large number of staff and children involved in a nursery school
makes it vital for the headteacher to organise routines and
duties carefully. She has to think of this when she takes on
students to train as nursery nurses.

The nursery class

A great deal of the new nursery education provision made since
1972 has been in the form of nursery classes attached to a
primary school. Your training in such a class would be similar
to that of a nursery school, except that the school will probably
be very much bigger and the nursery class may have fewer
children compared with a nursery school. You may perhaps
share the staff room for the whole school and so would meet a
larger number of teachers and staff.

The first school

Students training in a first school play a different role from
those training in a nursery school. The age of the children
makes the programme quite different, as more time will be
spent in formal educational activities. It is likely that you will
be given quite clear directions from the teacher you are placed
with. The sort of work involved depends somewhat on the
programme of the school and approach of the teacher. Most

students in first schools find themselves mixing paints, supervising craft tables, putting up displays and tidying and maintaining equipment. They also help the children in dressing, supervise them in cloakrooms and talk with them as they work and play throughout the day (Plate 5).

Plate 5. A student nursery nurse at a first school, Briar Hill, Leamington Spa, watching the children on the rope ladder.

You will work closely with the teacher, helping her in any way possible. The teacher will usually arrange for you to take small groups for special activities, including stories and craft (Plates 6, 7 and 8). You will need to learn to print well in the style which the school uses, in order that the children can see good examples if you label displays or write a word for them to copy.

Plate 6. Sharing the children's pleasure in balancing a model.

The day nursery

The student's role in a day nursery is again to work alongside the qualified staff. In this situation the staff will not be teachers but trained nursery nurses and sometimes nurses. The person in charge used to be called Matron but is now sometimes known as a Nursery Officer. The age of the children in the day nursery dictates the kind of routine which is established. There will be a great deal of time spent by staff in the daily care of the children, feeding, bathing and dressing them as needed. The hours of the day nursery are longer than a school day. They

Plate 7. Exploring together the properties of modelling material.

vary from place to place but may be from 8.30 a.m. to 5.30 p.m. and sometimes longer. The extra demands on staff in caring for the children usually means that there are more adults allowed per child. The children normally sleep for some part of the day and are sometimes taken out for walks in their prams. The longer day usually means that staff need more breaks from their duties with the children and the staff take turns for these and have a suitable room allocated for this purpose. They are sometimes given free meals while on duty. In some places this privilege is extended to students when they are with the children for meals but more often they pay a small amount towards their meals.

Plate 8. Taking a small group for a craft activity in a first school.

The residential home

Some students are able to have practical placement training in residential establishments. These are becoming fewer as more babies are placed in foster care but there are still some, mainly run by voluntary bodies. In the homes the staff training the nursery nurse student will usually be nursery nurses but they will sometimes have a residential social work background. The work the student does will be with the children and will vary according to the ages of the children.

Questions

1. Why is it important that a student should understand fully the working situation into which she goes for practical placement?

2. How can a student ensure that she is well received and fits in easily at practical placement?

3. 'Confidential' is a term we use about private information to do with children and families. Why is it important for a student to understand fully and abide by the code of confidentiality?

4. The student will have different duties according to where she is placed for practical experience. Describe some of these differences.

V

Observation of Children

NNEB syllabus requirements

The Board requires that you make observations of children over the two years as an integral part of your training. You might think that it would be impossible to work with children without observing them, but there are very differing degrees of observation, and the aim will be that you should gain an understanding of what you see in children's development and behaviour by watching them carefully. But first you must learn the skill of accurate observation and recording.

The basis of your vocational study will be the growth and

development of children. A record of observations must be kept by you in a concise and simple form. The significance of the observations made will be discussed by the student both with members of staff at practical placement and with tutors at college.

Your records of observations will be presented to the examiners as evidence of your work during the two years of training. Apart from the final examination, this may be the only written work which the examiners will have to go on in deciding if you should pass or fail, although it is possible the examiners will take other work into consideration. Observations should not be neglected, therefore, but should be a good reflection of what you have seen and understood during your training.

Your observations over the two years will take a number of forms. Each college gives advice and direction about how it wants you to go about making this record. Some colleges prefer that you start by learning the precise skills of observation first, and then proceed slowly towards more general observations. The ability to observe and record accurately is a skill which needs to be developed and will prove useful to you in all you do.

You may be asked, in your first term, to write quite general observations about the children you see in practical placement. As you proceed through the two years you will be helped to look at more specific activities (Plates 9 and 10) and to become more

Plate 9. A student nursery nurse at Lillington Nursery School, Leamington Spa, observing a teacher of the deaf (right) demonstrating language teaching.

Plate 10. The student observing with her tutor, the author (left) the hearing-impaired child playing in a group with other children.

adept at recording what you see correctly. Whenever you go on a visit to see children you should write up what you see and keep your notes for your file of observations.

Your college tutor may ask you to observe more than one child or watch some activity to see what different children do. You may also be asked to observe one child in a number of different situations and settings. Students are sometimes able to observe mothers and their babies. This involves arranging to visit a mother and her baby, or being visited at college by them, so that you can see and discuss how the baby is growing and developing. If you are placed for practical work where there are babies and toddlers, you may have the pleasure of recording babies' first teeth, first steps, etc.

At one college I have seen the students write an account of their own childhood. They enjoy talking with their parents about it, and find it interesting and helpful to look at their own development towards adulthood and what they think has affected their lives and their personalities.

It is very helpful if staff at practical placement read your records. Since they are seeing the same children and developments as you, they can tell you if you have recorded them accurately. So don't be afraid to ask for your work to be assessed, and listen carefully to any comments.

When you start working with children you may feel you have a good idea of what to expect because you have already had a lot of experience with young children. It is likely, however, that most students have had only a limited experience and this will make them unsure of what to expect in children's behaviour and how to react to them. If you are surprised at the things they do, you will be less able to respond correctly to help them or to know what to provide for them at their different stages of development. By studying how children behave for two years you will build up a good basis of knowledge about what to expect, about what is 'normal' (and a surprising number of things are) and what is out of the ordinary. In this way you will know what to do to help each child individually.

Use your observations of children to build up as factual a picture of their infinite varieties as possible. Avoid opinions and judgements in your record. You may wish to write comments separately, but approach the whole as a document of evidence, rather like a detective presenting a case. What you are looking for is evidence that your reading in child development is accurate and that you have recognised the various stages.

As a qualified nursery nurse you may in the future be required to supply accurate observations of children in your care to professionals who will use them in a diagnostic capacity. There is no room in such records for personal opinions, but there is a need for minute detail in describing what you have seen. Such accurate records are also helpful to others to look back on when they are checking progress in the future.

Use of language in reporting

Some people find written English difficult; others have a natural flair for it and find writing enjoyable. Undoubtedly we all, at some time or other, have to sit down and make ourselves write when perhaps we would much rather do something else or nothing at all. Self-discipline is just one more way that we learn and grow as people. Take this attitude when you feel like putting off your written observations.

Talking to friends and relatives about what you have seen will help you to put thoughts and impressions into words. Or put them into words in your own mind as you travel home on the bus — you can have quite interesting conversations with yourself with no fear of sounding silly! When you then come to write down what you have seen the words will be ready and waiting in your mind.

Descriptive writing can be fun and is very challenging. Imagine you are writing for someone who lives in Australia and knows nothing about the children you are writing about. Details such as colour, atmosphere, events and background should all build up into a whole picture. If you find this difficult, ask your Lecturer in English at college to give you some practice and help. Sometimes a visit to the zoo to observe the animals can be an exciting event to record and describe. Try recording your observations of a monkey for ten minutes!

Words are valuable tools. Used well they can affect our lives quite dramatically. How often have you wished after an event that you have not said something or that you had said the right words which would have shown what you really meant? Opportunities are often missed and as a result relationships and events are affected. So make words work for you, both verbally and in writing! To help yourself, write down all the ways you can think of that a child comes into a room: he bounces, leaps, shuffles, marches, creeps, dashes, ambles, saunters, struts, strolls, etc. Then try to describe happiness, sadness, talk, in the same way. Keep adding to your list so that you can refer to it for the right word from time to time.

Don't be afraid to adopt new words in your own conversation. You will be learning about the vocabulary of children and how it develops. Our own vocabulary continues to develop, as long as we are thinking people, throughout our lives. In fact, we understand many more words than we use ourselves. You may feel uncomfortable when you use a new word for the first time. The language doesn't seem natural and you may feel afraid to sound as if you are showing off. But next time you use it this will not be so, and from then on the word becomes one of your own. You may also feel pressure from your peers to conform to the group language usage. Remember that you are all students, studying and developing, extending yourselves, particularly in your ability to express yourself to others, and all should go well in your own language development as you work together.

Observations

Your college tutors will ask you to observe all kinds of activities of children. Each tutor and college has an individual method of directing students in this area, but to give you an idea, some of the things they may set for you to do might include the following activities.

Routines

Children's understanding of routines is very different from our own. Washing hands, for instance, is to us a means of ensuring cleanliness; to a child it can be a lovely opportunity to play with taps, soap and water, and as a result it takes a long time, or it can be an intrusive nuisance which delays the child's activity in some other area. Only gradually do children accept our routines as necessary, although for a long time they may not understand why.

Routine activities in which you may observe children in groups include dressing, toileting, washing, clearing up, sitting in a group.

Ask yourself the following questions about the routine. What was the stimulus for the activity? What was the setting? How does the child manage the routine? How did he look? What did the child do straight afterwards?

Note the time as you go along.

Use of materials

We can observe a great deal about a child in his response to materials. A child uses materials to express thoughts and feel-

ings about the world around him and his place in it. He sorts things out for himself as he plays. Typical materials which you will observe children using are clay, collage, sand and water.

Describe the setting, organisation and presentation of the material. How did he come to be playing with it? Who is with him or nearby? How does he use the materials? Include hand and body movements, facial expression, results, language used and the length of time his play takes in minutes. Why does the play come to an end? Where does he go to immediately afterwards?

Mealtimes

A great deal can be learned about children if you can observe them at mealtimes. There is a very close emotional relationship between a young child and his mother when it comes to eating. Since birth the child has been fed by mother and this has been one important way that she has cared for and loved the child. It is not surprising, therefore, that we often find a young child quite unprepared to stay to a nursery or first school meal, although he is happy for the rest of the day. The meal reminds him too much of her absence and his loss.

Each child eats differently according to his training. Differ-. ent demands are made upon him when sitting at the table. He needs manipulative skill when using implements and social maturity when conversing during the meal. Record facts as you observe.

Active play

Describe the apparatus and setting for the active play which you see. How did the activity start? What other children are involved? Describe the physical co-ordination and skill of the child. Are thought and problem solving in evidence? How does the action end? Is it carried on again later? How long does the play last?

Relationships with adults and children

You will notice that children respond differently to people just as we do. There may be a favourite friend, child or adult, and it will be interesting to see how the child manages social inter-course for himself. The same child may seem very different in his reactions from one situation to another because of the interaction of individuals and groups. You will find the response to mother, for example, will be different from the response to a member of staff. As you mention other children, record their ages in your notes so that the reader will have more information to go on.

Fatigue

Children behave very differently from usual when they are tired, so being able to notice tiredness in children is important. What evidence is there of fatigue? How does the child behave, and what is his physical appearance? If you can observe the same child when fresh and when tired you should be able to notice a contrast.

Remember to listen!

Observing children does not only mean watching them. It includes listening to the sounds they make. Your observations will be much richer if you can record what sounds take place as well as what you see. You may be able to use a tape recorder sometimes to catch conversations between children and between children and adults. You will in any case be able to remember some of the sounds, words or phrases used. This will, of course, include baby noises, whoops of joy and howls of rage or distress, so develop the use of all your senses when observing children and your own skills of recording will improve as you practise.

Contact with children other than at practical placement

Throughout your training you should take advantage of any extra contact that you have with young children and their families. In this way you will supplement your practical placement experience and extend your knowledge.

Your natural interest in children should prompt you to be alert to their activities. If you keep your eyes and ears open wherever you are, you will learn a great deal about children.

Informal contact with children
Private houses

Your college tutor may ask you to try to observe the same child in a number of different situations. At some time during your training you may be invited to a house where children live. Observations of the children you see on occasions like these will be helpful. Some colleges now make formal arrangements for such visits on a regular basis, as it is undoubtedly helpful for a student to see children in their own homes and to notice how they react with their own families. Whether formally arranged or incidental to you personally, such experience is very valuable. You will, perhaps, observe the child's relationship with his father as well as with his mother. You will notice quite different behaviour in the same child depending on where he is and who he is with.

Public playgrounds, supermarkets, school gates

Visits to public places such as playgrounds, supermarkets or school gates can offer excellent opportunities for you to observe children and there is the added convenience of being able to make them at any time. It is wise to set out with some ideas of events you might look for, but then you will also need to take advantage of what you find, wherever it happens to take place. If you visit a playground at various times during a week you will find that different people frequent it at different times and on different days. You will need to think about the adult/child relationships you see. Are the children with a parent? A grandparent? A childminder? Notice what each child does, about how old he seems, how long he plays in different areas and what contact he makes with the adult or other children. How does the weather affect the playground activities?

Large supermarkets offer interesting opportunities for observing children. What does a mother do with her baby when shopping? Has she more than one small child to care for while she shops? Is she able to talk to her toddler at the same time? Try to observe contrasts in approaches to children by parents. Some families seem relaxed and happy and others have screaming children to deal with. Notice the sort of food the families are buying. Do the items reflect a concern about the nutritional values of food?

If you can be outside a school when mothers come to pick up their children, it will be interesting for you to see the way the children come out. Do they rush to Mum or dawdle? Do they speak to or acknowledge their younger siblings in pushchairs? Do they look tired?

Are they proudly showing mother something they have made? Are they fully dressed? Have a look at the mothers. Are they talking to each other in a friendly fashion? Are they looking anxious and unhappy? Can you match the child with the parent before they come together?

You may see a child met by a grandparent. How is the

COUNTY
FIRST
SCHOOL

relationship working? Is the grandparent relaxed and happy? Permissive or strict? Is the child at ease?

Public transport provides informal opportunities to see children in action. The confined space makes it impossible not to overhear conversation and witness events. Children often chat to strangers in such situations.

You may also witness a young child with an older brother or sister. How does the older sibling manage?

Special visits

It is usual to place students in two different establishments for practical experience during the two years. Colleges can sometimes augment this experience by arranging visits of observation for students, though this depends very much on where the course is located and what other facilities are nearby.

These visits are helpful as they allow students to see the children in a large variety of situations. They also offer opportunities for students to see the variety of places in which nursery nurses work once they are qualified.

The course tutor at college will take a great deal of trouble to try to arrange these visits. Finding the time to fit them in with college timetables and practical placement is always difficult, especially as some of the places to visit will only be able to accept visitors at certain times. The people concerned are usually pleased to accept visits from nursery nurse students, but remember that as a visitor you are an extra item for them to consider and fit into their day. It is sometimes the case that visitors will upset the children concerned and this has to be borne in mind if arrangements are made for you. To give you an idea of the demands for visits which can be made on an establishment, consider this list of visitors to a nursery school, all made in one term:

parents, both present and future
local education authority officers and advisers
health visitor
school doctor
school nurse
school dentist
social worker
teacher from first school (to visit children going on to her)
nursery nurse students (other than those placed in this school)
student teacher (on school practice)
student health visitor
further education students (other than those on the NNEB course)
college tutors (NNEB course)
college of education tutors
secondary school pupils
secondary school teacher
foreign visitors.

You will see that this number of visitors could easily prove too much of a burden for a school and could begin to affect the programme for the children, especially where the head is a teaching head, as is often the case. The schools try, however, to cope with visits, partly because they are essential but also because they realise the important role of visits in training new people in work with children. They also believe it important to establish good relationships with all who are interested in their work.

Once you start work after you are trained it may be difficult for you to visit other places, so it is particularly important that you see as much as possible while you are a student. If you have visited a special school in a hospital, for instance, you will have very much greater knowledge of it than if you have just heard or read about it. Your training will be much more complete, and when the need arises for you to discuss anything about children in special schools you will be better prepared. So whatever happens, don't miss a visit that has been arranged for you if at all possible. It may be your only chance during your training, and so particularly difficult to make up in any way. Of course, if you have a bad cold, you must not visit anywhere where your germs could cause serious difficulty. If you are not sure about this, ask your health tutor, who will soon advise you.

The long list of visitors I have mentioned will show you that visitors are privileged and are welcomed at some cost into many establishments where children are cared for. You can make things easier for those you visit if you are thoughtful and considerate in your own behaviour. Remember that you represent your college on such visits and that in the future other students will want to visit.

The college tutors will give you some information about the place you are visiting. You will have lectures which deal with the various aspects of child care and so will have some introduction to the subject before you go. You may find, however, that the timing of lectures doesn't fit in with your visit and it would be wise, therefore, to see what you can find out for yourself beforehand. Some of your text books will refer to the variety of places you may visit, but if you can't find anything, ask your tutors.

When you arrive, if staff are busy too many questions can be a nuisance, so use your own judgement. You can look at the children and try to decide if they seem healthy. Does their hair shine? How are they dressed? Do they seem alert? Can you spot contrasts? Look at the equipment. Notice routines and how they are organised. Do parents come in, and do some stay?

You can also look at the location of the establishment. What kind of homes do the children live in? Is there a park nearby? How do the staff manage the children? How do the children react to you? What sort of traffic is there outside? Where are the nearest shops? Are there pets about?

Places you may visit to observe children in particular circumstances
Children's wards

You may have visited someone in hospital and seen that the comfort and safety of the patients is of paramount importance. The emphasis is on quiet and cleanliness, and as a visitor you must, of course, observe these aspects of hospital life.

Children in hospital are obviously under particular stress. They are surrounded by strangers and perhaps away from mother for the first time. They may also be feeling uncomfortable and ill. It is likely that any extra new people may be unwelcome, although in some cases the children will be glad of new company. A visiting student must be alert and sensitive in hospital and ready to respond to staff requests, whatever happens.

Maternity wards

Nursery nurse students love to visit maternity wards in hospitals and are delighted to see new-born babies (Plate 11). Take your directions from the midwifery staff nurse showing you around. Some mothers will want privacy. If you are allowed quite near to the babies, remember to be quiet. In some hospitals you will be asked to put on clean overalls (which the hospital provides) before going around the wards. If you are going to spend more than a short time on a ward, it is a good idea to take a clean overall with you and to wear shoes which are suitable. Make sure your hair is neat and your fingernails are short. If you are going to touch the babies you must follow the hygiene policy of the particular unit.

Special schools

You will find that special schools have a very friendly and welcoming atmosphere. The special needs of the children demand that they be in smaller groups and they receive a lot of individual attention. It is possible that the children will react to you differently from others you have met. You may see retarded children or children with disabilities such as deafness. You will certainly be able to notice differences in the children and it is

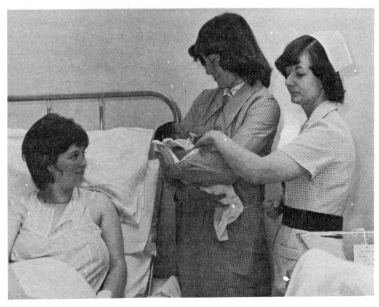

Plate 11. A student nursery nurse on a visit to the maternity unit at Warnford Hospital, Leamington Spa, holding a new baby, watched by the mother and a staff nurse.

wise to be prepared for this. They will often make big demands on your attention.

Health clinics

Your visits to clinics will allow you to see mothers and their children in various circumstances and the care which is provided under our National Health Service. You may visit a pre-natal clinic and be able to observe the care and education the mother receives both before and after the birth of her baby. You may also visit the well baby clinic to watch the regular check-ups given to babies and hear what questions are asked and what advice given. Remember that the mothers (and perhaps fathers) may feel they prefer privacy when discussing such matters, so be careful not to intrude where you shouldn't. The health visitor or nurse who has allowed you to come will tell you what to do and explain what is happening. It will be

interesting for you to see how very much babies differ even
when they are the same age.

Assessment centres

There are special centres which children attend for assessment
for a number of reasons, usually as a result of some difficulty
experienced by the child. At the centre the child is given tests to
measure his development and physical well being. Specialist
staff carry out such tests and you will often find a parent also
attending. It is usual to find nursery nurses working in such
centres.

After your visit be sure to write up some notes about it as
soon as you can, while it is still fresh in your mind. You may be
able to jot things down on your ride home on the bus. If there
are questions and opinions in your mind about something you
have seen, write these down as well. You will then be able to
remember them when you discuss the visit at college. A student
who has no comment after such a visit shows very little interest
in her work.

If you write up your visit well, it will be very helpful for you to
refer to later for use in your written work. It is also a good thing
to discuss your visit with a friend or your family. You will find
that if you tell someone where you have been and describe what

you have seen, it will mean you have a clearer picture of your visit in your mind, which will help you remember it in future. Explaining anything to someone else is always a good exercise in clarifying your own thoughts on the subject. If you can put things into words, you will find it easier when you come to write them down.

Questions

1. Why does the NNEB syllabus require that you undertake written observations of children?

2. Why is it important that a nursery nurse student should express herself well in spoken and written English? What sort of writing makes observations of children both interesting and useful?

3. It is important that you miss none of the special visits that your tutor arranges. Explain why this is so, and describe some of the places these visits might include.

4. Describe some of the opportunities to observe children which a student nursery nurse might come across when she is out on a Saturday afternoon.

5. Why is it important for student nursery nurses to make contact with children in varying situations? What is the best way to ensure that what is seen on such occasions is fully understood and remembered?

VI

Activities that You Will Come Across in Practical Placement

The world of young children in groups is quite different from anything you may have previously come across.

When you first arrive at your practical placement you will notice the child-sized equipment. Chairs and tables of the right size and storage shelves at a convenient height will be provided for the children to use. The bathroom will have mini-sized toilets and washbasins so that the children can manage easily. Mirrors will be placed where the children can see themselves. You may find that each child has his own individual towel, comb and toothbrush which are hung at the appropriate height, with a special picture that he can identify as his own. Some nurseries and schools now use paper towels, but, again, they will be within the children's reach. If the children use mugs, they may have their own individual ones. When children drink milk from a bottle with a straw, sometimes an identifying picture is looped over each bottle so that the staff know who has had his milk. You may be surprised at the independence of quite young children and how much they can manage for themselves, as they are encouraged to try to dress themselves, wash their hands and pour their own milk. Suitable equipment of the right size makes it easier for them to handle things and learn such skills, and all these routine activities have been planned to promote efforts towards independence on the part of the children.

Safety factors are considered when furniture and equipment are arranged in a room. It is likely that areas will be sectioned off for block play or messy activities.

Provision for easy clearing up and sorting of equipment will have been made. There will be a method of dealing with all contingencies, however they occur, including the wiping up of spills, changes of wet or dirty clothing and first aid for scrapes and bumps. Since the staff all know and have agreed on these procedures it is easy for them to be dealt with as they occur.

Plate 12. A student nursery nurse in the home corner at Lillington Nursery School talking to her tutor (standing).

The children's play needs will be met in a large variety of ways. There will be a quiet area set aside for the child who wants to withdraw and perhaps listen to a story or look at books. Music may be provided in some form or other, including radio, record player and instruments which the children may use themselves. Sand and water are often available to be played with and suitable overalls are provided, hung conveniently so that the children can help themselves. Children like to play at pretend games and there is frequently a wendy corner fitted out like a miniature house with all the relevant equipment, including dolls for the babies and a play cooker (Plate 12).

Plate 13. A nursery nurse at Warwick Nursery School enjoying the fun as the children blow bubbles outside in a covered, paved area.

When children are cared for in groups it is usual to find an outdoor play area which has been specially planned for them (Plate 13 and cover photographs).

The first thing you will notice is that it is safely enclosed with a gate that the children cannot open. Safety will also have been considered in the siting and design of the play equipment. A sand pit is an extremely popular provision often found outside. Staff may cover it at night — there will certainly be a variety of methods of doing this if you do see it. Some kind of climbing equipment is usually available so that the children can try out and develop their physical skills. Large-wheeled toys are popular and often involve the children in co-operative play, in which they help each other by pushing and pulling. Some of the outside area will be grass-covered and some paved. Fortunate groups may have outdoor space with a cover overhead for use in inclement weather. Pets may be kept outside for the children to feed and play with (Plate 14). The staff will have agreed routines for the supervision of the children's play outside as they do inside.

Each day different activities will be provided in addition to the play activities mentioned. Staff will have their own way of organising and directing such activities and you will learn how and why as you watch. The nursery nurse student will need to learn every aspect of what goes on and how things are done in her practical placement.

The student's involvement in practical placement activities

The opportunities offered to students in practical placements vary a great deal because of the different organisations and ages of the children. Each establishment will offer special areas of experience from which the student can learn different skills. It may be that she will become expert at changing nappies and feeding babies in one nursery; she may then find that these skills are unused in her next practical placement but she will learn something else which is new. Many different skills are needed by a nursery nurse and each is just as important in its own way as the others.

Plate 14. A student nursery nurse helping to feed the guinea-pig.

The presentation of activities to groups of children

The example of the staff will teach you a great deal about how to present activities to the children. The following points should be considered.

(a) Think carefully about how activities are presented. Of course, you will not be expected to be able to initiate activities on your first day, but you should be ready to try as soon as possible. The skills are built up through practice, and if things are done regularly, you will improve as you go along. Don't hang back at first because of lack of confidence. The way to learn is through doing, so plunge in and have a go.

(b)   Remember that students' 'practice' has to be fitted into the normal routine of the children, so consultation with the teacher or nursery nurse in charge is necessary. Ask if and when you may do something, and also discuss your plans with whoever is in charge and ask if they think them suitable. Their advice will be invaluable, as they will have a pretty good idea of what activities are successful and how best to present them. But do not always wait for suggestions from them. They may be pleased to hear new suggestions from you.

(c)   You may wish to keep a note book or card file of plans you make and to jot down comments afterwards as to how the planned activity went and what follow-up may be necessary. Ask yourself how you will do it next time.

(d)   Think carefully about the age of the children. Whatever you plan to do must offer something suitable to their stage of development and must have some overall aim.

Attitudes and atmosphere

When you plan and carry out a special activity for children you must take care to approach the children in the right manner. Your enthusiasm will promote interest in the children, but if you are too enthusiastic, you will excite them and this will not be helpful! You may find that too many children will want to participate immediately. The children will be learning that they must take turns to do things, and the staff will be keeping a record so that no child is left out and they all have an opportunity to join in at some time. You will need to consult with the staff about which children you should ask to join you and how many.

If you take a great deal of care in planning and carrying out an activity, you will find that the children soon learn to expect an interesting and enjoyable experience in your company and will respond with pleasure to you. Poorly prepared and dull, repetitive activities will soon lose the children's interest and you will find that they wander off to other activities which they find more absorbing. Make sure, therefore, that the children soon learn that the things they do with you are interesting and worth while.

You will have been talking and thinking at college about why children do certain things and how they develop as they grow. This should help you to recognise what they need. Try to remember these things in carrying out activities with children so that you bear in mind all the time what your aims are and can see whether they are being achieved.

Activities to present to children
Cooking

Deciding what to cook will be the first task. There are a large number of cookery books for children nowadays but a lot of them are full of recipes for sweets and foods which are mainly carbohydrate. If you think about what you are learning about nutrition in your lectures at college, you will realise how impor-

tant it is to train children away from eating sweets and too many carbohydrates. You may find that the children you work with know very little about fresh fruits and vegetables. If you find a way of introducing these foods that is fun, the children will be learning important new tastes which may have an effect on their eating habits and, ultimately, their health. Keep this in mind when you are looking for recipes. (Of course, you must also think of cost and the availability of fresh foods according to the seasons.) Demonstrate to the children that eating the right foods can be fun.

When you have decided what cooking activity you wish to do, discuss it with the staff. Be ready to give some reasons for your choice and also some indication of how you plan to carry it out. Although we call this activity 'cooking', it may in fact only involve preparation of food, as quite a lot can be done with children which is interesting and does not need actual cooking. Prepare the children beforehand quietly by inviting them to join you. Tell them what you are planning to do and talk about food and cleanliness. Why do we wash our hands before cooking? Why do we wear a special apron and not the aprons we use for painting? (Incidentally, if your school needs some cooking aprons, you could perhaps make a set for them.) You will have all the ingredients and dishes which you need ready to hand and will have thought about what the children can manage to do themselves. They will soon be bored if they have to just watch all the time, so try to plan that each has something to do (Plate 15). They will enjoy weighing and measuring different ingredients. It is better to have individual bowls for each child to mix in than one large one for them all. Don't be afraid to let children cut up apples or carrots with knives. Show them how to do it safely, and with your supervision and help they will enjoy being allowed to try. They will also like grating vegetables and cheese. Young children may not have had the opportunity to look at and discuss food in its different states. I remember a two-year-old saying 'That's not potatoes' when he saw them dirty and unpeeled! Think of all the different ways a potato can look, feel and taste, and you will see that little children have a lot to learn about what we take for granted.

It might be a good idea to go to the local shop with the children to buy the ingredients for your cooking. Going shopping with you will be another activity that the children will learn from. This will need extra planning and perhaps assistance from another member of staff. We usually include four to six children in a cooking session and with this number you would need two adults to go to the shop. You can talk about the traffic and other things you see, about the money and where the food comes from before it gets to the shop, etc. This kind of visit to a shop with you will be different from the children's usual shopping with mother, as your visit will be centred on the

Plate 15. Children at Warwick Nursery School making jam tarts guided by a nursery nurse.

children and you will be helping them rather than getting your own shopping done.

While you are cooking with the children try to get them to think about what they are doing by asking questions and discussing what you are all doing. 'I wonder how it will taste?', 'This is a pretty green colour,' 'What do you think will happen?' are the sort of questions and comments you can make. Conversations about home, where mummy and daddy cook and grow vegetables in the garden, will all prove interesting to the children and will doubtless prompt plenty of comments from them. If you do use a cooker, remember safety factors. It is much better to train children to understand what dangers there are than just to tell them not to do something. If they have a reason and know there is a danger, they are more likely to be able to take care of themselves when necessary. But with a group of children it will be your job to ensure that safety is remembered. Always try to let the children see you taking things out of the oven or cooking on the top of a stove. The change that takes place in food because of heat is an early science experience for the children. If you just tell them you put the food in the oven, it will not be the same as if they actually see it being done.

Sometimes it is arranged that children take home what they have made at the nursery, and this includes cooking. It might be more fun to let them eat it together, in a little group, since there is a danger that you might be more concerned about an end product that looks good enough to take home than the enjoyment and learning experience of the children. You will have much more scope in choice of cooking activity, too, if the things do not have to be transported home. The timing of your cooking will have to be considered. If it takes place in the afternoon, the children can eat the things for their tea before going home. A part-time morning session may be more difficult, as you will not want the children to eat just before lunch. Try to have the morning cooking session early, so that the food could be eaten as a mid-morning break. Also, plan on a very small helping for each child, so that it is just a little tasting ceremony. Small amounts of tasty food can be much more fun than a big plateful to a small child. You might think about how to serve the food attractively. Let the children help you to make the table pretty with a tablecloth and a centrepiece made by them out of flowers or twigs and grasses from the nursery garden.

As you will see, so many activities can grow out of your initial plan to 'do cooking', and this is the case with all activities with children. You must be alert to all the learning opportunities the children are offered and must at all times promote the children's language and thinking by talking to them and stimulating a dialogue.

Art and craft

Young children are naturally interested in any new experience and when they attend a nursery they are usually delighted with the provisions made for them to paint, paste and cut out. Often such opportunities will not have been available to them at home or in such comfortable and convenient surroundings. The modern house is usually limited in space and easily cleaned floors are often confined to the kitchen and bathroom. This should not discourage anyone from providing messy activities at home, however, as children gain a great deal from playing with such materials and the peaceful and productive time is often very well worth the necessary cleaning up which follows. In fine weather the garden is an ideal place.

When children are working with creative materials it is important to allow them to express themselves freely as they wish. You have only to look at a young child's drawing to see how completely individual it is. This unique quality is one of the essentials in creative work, and so there is little value in the child producing something that an adult has thought of. The adult's role in creative activities is to provide a large variety of interesting materials in a suitably comfortable setting so that the children will want to use them. Work done in this way will be different from each child.

In some nurseries and schools staff may have slipped into the habit of wanting the children to produce an end product for them to take home. When the child starts at the nursery there is a very real link formed for the child when he paints a picture and then takes it home. This is tangible evidence of the new fact that he has spent time away from mother and has had some measure of success in operating as a separate individual from her. There is, therefore, a very understandable emphasis put upon such a painting, but it is unfortunate if this develops into or continues to be the only link between nursery and home. Staff should talk to the mother when she picks up the child, for instance about how he has been playing with the bricks for a long time, so that she comes to hear and talk about all the other activities and doesn't just look for a 'product' as evidence that he is all right away from her. The attitude of the staff is all-important in this question of art and craft activities. Too often one finds that an adult has done a great deal of the work to 'make' something and although the children are amused and pleased to say 'Look what *I've* made', great care must be taken to avoid such activities becoming merely time-fillers to keep children occupied. Children's natural drive to do things will occupy them much more beneficially, as they will practise skills and develop their own individual potential if given the right opportunities.

So whatever art and craft activities you plan, keep these points always in mind. If you find you end up exhausted after an afternoon of producing masks for the children which they were supposed to be making, it is likely that you are on the wrong track. If you want to make something for the children (for example, hats for a party) and there is no reason why you shouldn't, make them on your own in peace and quiet. If you want the children to make something, be quite sure it is within their own capabilities and that any assistance you have to give is minimal.

Organisation is important when you are presenting art and craft materials to little children. It is likely that the nursery has a very definite organisation already, which all the staff know and keep to, but don't be afraid to suggest innovations or to produce new material which you have thought of or seen elsewhere. New ideas are always welcome (although some may not suit the nursery you are in); don't feel hurt or offended if your idea is rejected. Also, remember your ideas for another place and time when perhaps you will be able to carry them out.

Every student soon finds that mixing powder paints and cleaning paint pots is a job she is given. It may well be the first one. Make sure you mix the paints well so that they are not too thick or too thin. In some nurseries a little paste powder is used to thicken the consistency of the paint but this can dull the brightness of the colours if too much is used. If your nursery does not have non-spill pots, only fill the paint pots half-way.

You can make non-spill paint pots yourself. Cut off the top quarter of a liquid detergent bottle; cut off about another quarter of the bottle and discard; then invert the top and push it into the bottom of the bottle (figure 9).

Another method of presenting paints is to use a square tin (the type which some powder paints come in), and make holes in each corner for a paint brush, so that four children can use the same colour. If you are using the solid tempera block paints, the block can be stuck on to the middle of the lid and the tin filled with water (figure 10). This kind of paint pot is particu-

Fig. 9   Improvised non-spill paint pot

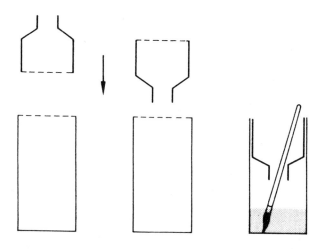

Fig. 10   Presenting paint

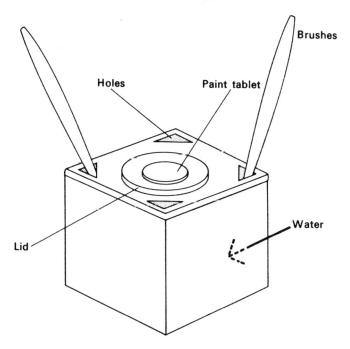

larly suitable if the children are working at a table, though the block paints are usually offered to school-age children, as at nursery age it is better if powder paints are mixed for them.

Paste is also presented in a variety of ways. If rubber-solution glue is used, it is usually put into disposable yoghurt cartons in small amounts, as it is difficult to clean out of jars. Sometimes paste is put on a small sponge in a shallow plastic container, but this makes the children's fingers sticky right from the start, which is difficult for them. Paste brushes and spreaders are also used, and the children will need to learn by watching how much paste is needed to stick things. It is something they will only learn from experience, so don't worry if there seems to be paste everywhere, including on top of what has been pasted down! Have a damp cloth handy for wiping sticky fingers when requested, but don't bother the children by insisting on cleaning them and the table all the time. If you know it is going to be a particularly messy time, it might be as well to ask the children to put on aprons as inevitably hands get wiped on clothes.

When you provide printing with paints put the paint in a shallow container with a sponge sitting in it. This way the children can press on the sponge and then onto their paper. It will be interesting to see what a variety of printing materials you can collect for yourself during your student years. Look out for things and try them yourself to see if they work well.

Finger painting is a lovely experience for little children. They sometimes approach the messiness with caution but soon thoroughly enjoy the sensations in conditions in which they are allowed to make a mess. Make sure sleeves are very well pushed up before they start and, of course, cover them up with aprons. Finger painting is most successful done straight onto a formica-topped table. Start with one colour and spoon on a generous amount in one spot. As the children get used to the medium, they can if they want make a 'print' of their pictures by pressing a piece of paper down onto the table. Sometimes children finger paint directly onto paper, but it will have to be strong and shiny for the paint to slip about without tearing the paper. This may mean expensive paper will be needed but there is really no need for it, as you will see. Finger paint can be bought ready made, but there are various methods of making ordinary paint suitable for finger painting. One way is to mix a lot of paste and powder paint together so that a thick solution is made. This will do, but sometimes the colour is not as exciting as it should be, as it becomes rather dull. Another way is to mix a thick starch solution. This takes some time and effort but the results can be excellent and it is doubtless cheaper than buying finger paint.

In some nurseries I have seen a liquid starch solution put on a surface with a sponge and then dry powder paint sprinkled on for the children to mix themselves with their fingers, which, of course, they enjoy.

When you start any activity with the children make sure that you have prepared all the things you will need beforehand and that you are ready to present them in a sensible way so that the children can all reach what they want for themselves. The best organisation will mean that they need little help from you to get on. It's a good idea to put the child's name on his work before he starts but don't make the name obtrusive. It is best to put it on the back so that the child has a clean paper to start − imagine how you would feel if you had to start writing an essay on paper that someone else had already written on.

Any of the above activities should be done with small groups of four to six children. When you talk with the children about their work, try to make comments which will help them. 'That's lovely' is an all too common remark. If you try to be truthful in your remarks and describe what you see, it could help the children to be discriminating in their own thoughts about their work. So 'You've worked a long time on that' or 'This is rather like the picture you did yesterday, but it has something else in it' may stimulate the children and will also show them that you are truly interested in what they do. When you have established a good relationship with a child it should also be possible to be critical in a friendly way, so that the child begins to see his own work as a reflection of his efforts. Then when high praise is given he will know that it is truly deserved and will enjoy the pleasure of real accomplishment.

Presenting modelling materials

Some type of modelling material is usually out at all times in a nursery school. Plasticine is sometimes used but it is the least satisfactory medium for young children. If it is to be used, make sure to soften it up before the children use it, as otherwise it is much too hard for them to manipulate. If it is kept in a warm place, it will be softer. I have seen hard bits of plasticine being used for cutting practice with scissors.

Clay is more suitable for little children and a very much more satisfying medium to work with. To keep clay soft while stored, shape it into a ball about the size of a grapefruit and press your thumb into it to make a hole. Pour a little water into the hole. Store the clay balls in a bin with a lid (they can also be covered with damp sacking to keep them really moist). This method is convenient, as the clay is ready, in the right amount, for presenting to the children the next time. Make sure they wear aprons when using the clay. It is a good idea to vary the presentation of the clay. Sometimes provide tools which can cut and make patterns. At other times let the children see what they can do with only their hands. Boards may not be necessary, as clay does no harm to formica-topped tables, but some establishments use boards if the table tops are wooden or the children are using implements.

Dough is a very popular material for children to manipulate. It can be made in various ways to give different effects, and it can be coloured with paint. The children can help mix it. To make dough you mix flour, salt and water. Start with a cup of flour and about half a cup of salt. The salt makes the mixture firm, holds the moisture and acts as a preservative so that the dough, if kept in a plastic bag in a cool place, will be usable for about a week or so. You will find you get different sorts of dough if you use self-raising flour sometimes and plain flour at others. Self-raising flour produces a stretchy elastic type of dough, which is lovely to pull and squeeze. It will not be so suitable for modelling shapes but this will not matter, as the children will enjoy finding out how it will behave. If you add powder paint to the dough after it is mixed, there will be an attractive marbling effect which the children can then gradually mix in as they work with the dough. You can also add a little cooking oil if you want to make it smooth and soft for the children. Another way to change the dough is to add something to it to give a different texture. Sand, lentils or rice make the dough gritty and bumpy. You might keep some smooth dough handy for the children to contrast the textures. Commercial play dough is a pleasant modelling medium but will be quite expensive to provide in large amounts. Remember to give each child a generous amount of any modelling material, at least the size of a grape-fruit. This activity usually gives rise to a lot of conversation which an adult can contribute to and develop.

Whenever you present these materials to children make sure you clean up really well afterwards. You will not be popular with staff or caretaker if you leave bits of clay or dough on the floor or messy cloths in the sink.

Puppet making

You will probably make different types of puppets at some time or other during your training. The first ones may be puppets that you make yourself to entertain the children and for them to play with. The second may be the puppets that the children can make themselves without too much help from you. Ping-pong balls stuck on a child's finger can be very effective if a piece of fabric is first draped over the hand. The child can stick bits of wool, felt and buttons on it to make a face and hair, or felt tip pens can be used to draw on a face. The age of the children will affect greatly how much they are able to do themselves.

Simple puppets can also be made from socks. You might like to prepare them for the children beforehand by cutting a mouth in the toe of the socks and sewing in some red material. The socks should be discarded child-sized socks.

The children can stick on fabric, felt and wool to make the sock puppets' faces. You can make some very effective puppets yourself this way. If they are sewn, they will last longer and be more effective. The results are always great fun. You can use a puppet in your story-telling sessions and the children will quickly have the puppets 'talking' to each other.

Books and storytime

Children enjoy looking at books and hearing stories from the age of one year. If they are read to and shown books from this early age it will mean that books are a normal part of their lives and they will accept books as something which afford a great deal of pleasure. Some children are not fortunate enough to have parents who read to them, and it is even more important, therefore, to provide attractive books and storytelling activities for them in the nursery (Plate 16).

Plate 16. Discussing a story.

During your training you must familiarise yourself with as many children's books as you can. This should not be difficult as they are very enjoyable to read. After some time you will come to have your own favourites but you will soon be impressed by the very large variety that is available. You may have a collection of children's books at your college and there will also be some at the practical placement. But there is no reason why you shouldn't go to the local children's library to browse and borrow as you please.

You may find that reading to one child is relatively easy and it is a very pleasant time for both child and adult. Reading to a group of children is, perhaps, more daunting a prospect for a student and is something you will undoubtedly get better at the more practice you have. Students are often anxious about keeping the children quiet and controlling the group. Confidence will come with time, so you must take every opportunity offered to practise reading to children and telling them stories. If you work at this over the two years of your training, your accomplishment will be something you can offer to children no matter where you work with them. A good story told well will hold the children's attention and the problem of control is solved.

There are some simple rules to keep in mind as you start to plan a story session.

1. Make the story so absorbing that the children will sit quietly because they want to hear you.

2. Choose a story which is suitable for the age group you are reading to. Are the pictures large enough for a group? Should you show the pictures? If so, should it be as you go along or at the end?

3. Practise and prepare the story very carefully beforehand. Read it aloud at home so that you become really familiar with it and decide how you will emphasise some parts. If you have a tape recorder, you might tape yourself and play it back to see how you sound. This can be quite an unpleasant shock the first time, but at least you will see how you need to improve and you can then wipe the tape clean! Your voice will need to be projected more to a group than if you are reading to one child on your lap, but once you are into the story, dropping your voice to a very quiet level at some points will add drama and excitement. Make sure the story has a good ending and avoid trailing off.

4. Make sure, too, that the children are settled before you start. Have they been to the toilet? Try to arrange as little

distraction in the room during the story as possible. Make the story just long enough for the children to practise sitting and listening in a group, but short enough so that when you finish they have not lost interest and started to fidget. It is much better to end storytime with the children wanting more, so that the next time they will come to listen to you eagerly. It is a good idea to start off with a little finger rhyme or song which the children know, to gain their attention. Try to arrange seating in which the children are comfortable. If they are too crowded, they will fidget.

5. Learn by heart a number of traditional and modern stories which you can then tell to children at any time. It is very good for children to listen to a story without pictures. They will imagine the 'pictures' for themselves, just as we do when we read a good book.

A story can be told to a child on a bus, in the bath or in the middle of the night when you don't want to put the light on, but want to reassure a frightened or sick child while he goes back to sleep. Here is a list of traditional stories which every nursery nurse should know by heart:

> The three little pigs
> Goldilocks and the three bears
> The gingerbread man
> Jack and the beanstalk
> The three billy goats gruff
> Henny penny
> Cinderella
> Chicken little
> The tale of the turnip

As you become more adept at telling stories you will find that you can make up your own stories for special occasions or to suit a particular situation. Children love to hear stories about themselves and the things they have done recently or are going to do in the near future. In this way you will help the children to put their experiences into words, using language to recount the past and project into the future. These activities are very important pre-reading activities for the children.

Visits and outings

As a student it is unlikely that you will be responsible for planning and organising a visit or outing with a group of children at a nursery or school, but during your training you must consider how these are arranged and carried out. You may be fortunate enough to go on a visit or outing with some children during your training.

There is great value in taking the children on visits. They find the outing very stimulating, even though they may have been to the same place before with their family. It is quite different going somewhere with their friends in a group, and the adults will be thinking of the children particularly and how to cater for their needs and interests.

A visit may be planned just for fun (for example, a walk to a nearby park to feed the ducks), but it will undoubtedly provide a great deal to talk about and will be an experience the children will have in common afterwards. Some visits may be planned with a special end in mind (for example, a trip to the shops to buy pet food for the nursery pets). Sometimes staff use a visit to stimulate the children's play at the nursery. If block play is not as constructive or absorbing to the children as it might be, a visit to a place where the children can observe bridges and road junctions may well provide just the stimulus to their play which is needed. If you are near an airport or a railway station, these too can prompt a great deal of constructive and imaginative play.

The accessibility of such exciting places is very important. Little children cannot enjoy outings if they involve long, tiresome journeys. What value there is in such an outing is lost if the children are too tired to enjoy it.

When you do go on outings try to include one adult to two children. (This may vary, of course, with the age of the children. Two 2-year-olds could be too much for one adult, but three 5-year-olds could be managed.) If you do have to travel with young children, it is a good idea to be prepared. Don't rely on being able to buy suitable food and drink on the way. Drinks and food will refresh the children when they need it and without delay. Avoid sickly foods! Try to plan for a quiet sit-down some time during the outing so that you can all rest. Take a damp facecloth in a plastic bag for wiping hot faces and sticky fingers while you are travelling. If you should have to be sitting still for long periods on a journey, plan things to keep the children occupied. Tell stories, play games, talk about what you see out of the windows, provide drawing materials or small toys. Space all these things out over the time so that something new is offered as the children get restless.

You may find the children don't want to talk about their outing as soon as they return. They may, instead, want to come to terms in their own minds with what they have done and seen. Don't be surprised, therefore, if some days later you see drawings, building play or imaginative activity which link up with your visit. It is best not to force comment from the children. You may have heard about the girl on a school outing, who remarked to her friend on the bus, 'Whatever you do, don't look out of the window or we'll have to write a composition on it when we get back.' The same feeling might well apply to little children, but they cannot put it into words and may just feel uncomfortable if pressed.

You can prompt continued interest, however, as long as it is done with tact and sensitivity. Putting up a picture of a place similar to that which you have visited may cause comment. Providing a book about the subject might also help. The adult provides the stimulation but it is often the case with little children that an unplanned incident, for example, a furry caterpillar found by a child, is more interesting to them. As a nursery nurse you must take advantage of both planned and unplanned activities to talk to the children and extend their thinking about their experiences. You must also train yourself to respond positively to insects and small animals that children come across! Remember that the children may adopt your attitudes and also your fears, so keep this in mind.

Music and singing

Young children respond naturally to music and it is a source of great pleasure to most of us. Regular music sessions are an important part of the curriculum in nursery and infant schools, and if you work with younger children you will find that they also respond to music at a very early age. The use of a lullaby to sing a baby to sleep is an effective means of relaxing the baby or child. If you are comforting a crying baby you may find you are rocking it and cooing to it in a soothing way which is quite an instinctive reaction on your part. Some people use music boxes or quiet records to relax their children before sleep.

Music should be used frequently in a nursery so that the children are able to hear different types and varieties. There are many children's records available now but sometimes you may find other records more suitable. It's worth looking out for records in jumble sales or second-hand stalls. A brass band playing marching songs, or old music hall songs, may prove very popular with the children. It is good if you can provide the right music to accompany children when they are playing make-believe — does the 'bride' want a wedding march played? Do the cowboys want some galloping music?

Children enjoy rhythm. As soon as they can stand up you will often see them bobbing up and down to a beat. This is something which can be developed with children in a group. You can clap rhythms for them to listen to and use shakers and instruments to produce a variety of loud, soft, quick and slow sounds and rhythms. Let the children experiment for themselves. They will enjoy singing songs and using such instruments at the same time.

When you teach children a new song be sure to make the words clear and understood. Adults find childish mistakes very amusing but our aim should be to teach the right words from the outset. When you start a new song try to sing it over at least once a day for a week so that the children learn it thoroughly.

Try to build up your own repertoire of songs throughout your training. You should also collect your own records and instruments for children so that you have something to offer wherever you go as a nursery nurse.

There is some disadvantage in having a radio on all the time with music playing. Children will not listen to it actively and it will be just background noise which is ignored but will disturb other thoughts and activities. Think of the difference in meaning between 'hear' and 'listen'. The first is done involuntarily and naturally; the second suggests active participation and concentration. Listening can be called a skill. How often does your mind wander when you should be listening to a lecture?

This skill of listening can be built up by practice and is one of the things children can learn with your help. An important fact to remember is that none of us listens carefully unless what is happening is interesting or of importance to us. Remember this when you ask children to listen.

Poems and rhymes

Children enjoy rhymes and often learn them as soon as they start to talk. Nursery rhymes are part of our culture and we say them to little children in a rhythmic way to amuse them. Make sure you know them all and use them often. Some children will not have heard them at home, particularly immigrant children whose parents are non-English-speaking.

Nonsense rhymes are great fun for children. They offer another way of getting children to listen to words and sounds and also to memorise them, as rhyme and rhythm make things easier to learn. Counting rhymes teach numbers and finger play and action rhymes fascinate the children as they try to participate.

Compiling a collection of ideas and items for future reference

As previously mentioned, your student years are a time when you should be building up a store of knowledge about children and how to provide suitable activities for their needs. Set out from the start to collect ideas and keep them for your future use. Learn stories, songs and rhymes and write down all kinds of activities you come across or do with the children. A record of the activities you do will serve as a reminder for you in future.

Think about how you .want to keep this information. You could assemble a file with sections marked off for different topics. A note book is useful but less practical if you want to add or take away a page. A card file is worth considering, as it is convenient to be able to remove the card you want to use and replace it after the activity with the children. A large file can become too cumbersome for easy use when you are working with children, so think about size, layout and presentation. A good collection will serve you as reference matter for many years, so the more care you take in collecting suitable material and information the less searching you will have to do in the future.

The activities discussed in this chapter should form a base for your collection. You can add anything you wish to it. You may want to collect a list of useful addresses, some pamphlets on places to visit with children, a list of good reference books, some pictures which tie in with the activities, etc. This collection will take some time for you to compile. You will be able to jot down ideas which occur to you when you go on visits to all kinds of establishments where children are gathered.

But don't spend so much time on it that there is no time left for you to learn by heart, practise and carry out the ideas. Whatever you do, don't spend hours copying out stories and poems from books when the title of the book would be sufficient for you to know where to find it. You will want to buy some books for your own use with children but don't rush to buy the first ones you see. Books will be available for you to borrow and use from college and from your practical training placement. If there is only one item in a book you want, then jot it down, but if you find a book you use often which contains many of the things you need, then it is obviously wise to buy it or ask for it as a Christmas or birthday present.

Whilst you are training it will be natural for you to 'collect' things. Anyone who works with children never throws anything away without thinking first of how children might use it. Scraps of material for collage, old clothes, shoes and hats for dressing up, boxes and cartons for handwork — all these could be invaluable, though ingenuity is sometimes required to think of how something can be used by or converted for children!

Collect pictures, also, from discarded magazines, calendars or brochures. Be selective so that you don't have too many. Choose really interesting pictures which you can see will have some purpose when you show them to children. If you think about children's play and activities, you will be able to see the sorts of pictures which will be interesting: block play — pictures of construction work, roads, airplanes, ships, trains; wendy house play — pictures of families at home, weddings, hospitals; cooking — there may be a spot where pictures of cooking could be put up. You could use a picture to make up a story. Mount the pictures on card, if possible, so that they will last. A clear coat of varnish will help to preserve them or plastic sheeting can be used. Don't be disheartened, however, if the cost of such mounting is so high that it is impractical. Try to keep all your pictures in a large flat folder until you can use them and keep replacing them as you go along with new ones.

Questions

1. Name five points that the student nursery nurse must consider when planning and preparing activities to carry out with young children.

2. What can children learn from their early involvement with food preparation and cookery?

3. Why is it important to remember the special abilities of the children when planning craft activities?

4. How can we ensure that children develop a real interest in books and stories? Why is it important for them to do so?

5. In what ways can a nursery nurse use music with children? How can a student develop an ability to provide such music?

Appendix A

The National Nursery Examination Board Syllabus

1. Contents of course

The following syllabus has been framed to give guidance to those responsible for the course. It is expected that each college will devise its own curriculum, though a brief outline of the areas of study to be covered is indicated below. Full account needs to be taken of the young people themselves, their stage of development, the areas of knowledge already explored and the skills they have acquired.

Students should be taught what young children are like at different stages in their growth and development and how they should be cared for. They will gain their knowledge through observation and through their practical work with children, through lectures, by discussion with those concerned in both the theoretical and practical training and through suggested lines of reading. Records of students' practical experience will be kept.

2. Observation of children

As observation of children forms an integral part of the training from the start, the following notes on the making of the student's record may be helpful.

Students will have opportunities to observe how children behave and how they change. This growth and development will be the basis of the study. It is expected that students will find opportunities of supplementing their planned practical experience of young children by informal contacts with those they know.

The records kept by students should be simple and concise. The significance of the observations should be discussed by the students with members of staff both in the practical training placement and at college.

3. Child care and development (theory and practice)

The aim is to give nursery students a wide theoretical knowledge and understanding of children's growth, development and needs, and to combine this with practical knowledge to enable them after qualifying to care for young children in an appropriate manner wherever they are working.

The following areas of knowledge will need to be studied during the course:

(a) Development of the individual. Detailed study of the care of children and understanding of their development from 0−7 years to include physical, intellectual, emotional and social aspects.

(b) Needs of young children and their families, including social, physical, emotional and intellectual deprivation, physical handicap or illness, and disturbed behaviour and mental handicap. Those responsible for children must consider the means whereby the children's needs are met. As well as everyday matters such as food, shelter, clothing and other physical provisions, children need opportunities for play and language development, for companionship and the sharing of interests and activities. Most of the students' experience will be with normal healthy children, but variations in development will also have to be discussed.

(c) Students should realise the importance of continuity of individual care for the child, and the need for responsive, confident relationships among the members of the caring team.

(d) A knowledge of health matters and the health needs of children, such as good nutrition, the prevention and control of spread of infection (from day to day and during an outbreak), the prevention of accidents, elementary first aid, and simple steps which can be taken when a child is unwell or convalescent. Personal hygiene; the need for exercise and rest. Detailed consideration should be given to measures which are primarily for the individual and to those which become additionally essential when children are cared for in groups.

(e) The significance of the family as a social institution. The child, his home and the community. Present social trends, living conditions both urban and rural. Aspects of family life which provide for the sound development of the child in twentieth-century society. Awareness of ethical and spiritual values. Changes in the upbringing of children. Cultural patterns. Introduction to school life and what this means to the child and his parents. The nature and meaning of parental responsibility.

(f) An understanding of the education, social and health services, and community development. The responsibility of the professionally qualified person to the community.

Some of the above areas will involve a theoretical knowledge only; others will marry theory and practice.

4. The students' responsibility throughout training

It is expected that the responsibility given to students will increase throughout the two years, although they will work under the guidance of experienced staff members, each of whom has a contribution to make. It is important that students should feel themselves to be members of a group of people caring for children and that they follow the working pattern of the establishment in which they are placed.

It is important that throughout the course students should appreciate the underlying aims and development of the training so that in their turn they may contribute to the training of other students and young assistants.

They will become aware of the quality of personal relationships within a group and the effect of these on the well-being of both children and adults. Children need the companionship of lively minds and it is hoped that students will take every opportunity to enrich their own interests. They should be encouraged to extend their own understanding through reading and through development of their own creative abilities. A course of general studies enabling them to do this could be devised in such a way that consideration of the nature of man, the value of life, the wonders of nature and the place of the arts and sciences in human life and progress could all be presented to help towards both a personal enjoyment of living and a philosophy of life.

5. General studies

The proposals for this area are based on the belief that any scheme of vocational training should have a wider aim than the mere mastery of the processes involved. The main objective of general studies is the personal development of the student − a furthering of the student's education. On occasions, however, the general study can and should at one and the same time complement the vocational study.

The content of the course is divided into three broad areas in order to encourage integration and to achieve greater cohesion.

Integrated studies could develop through a thematic approach, but it is not envisaged that all areas or subjects would be involved on all occasions in developing a theme or topic or be involved to the same degree. It is not suggested that the entire scheme should revolve around themes and topics − but they are very appropriate on many occasions. It is hoped that each area of study will receive a reasonable allocation of time, but in planning the course it is not essential to have all areas offered concurrently − shorter, concise periods might be more valuable. In some colleges 'blocking of time' might be possible.

The three main areas are:

a. Communication and the creative arts
b. Man and his environment
c. Home and society.

a. Communication and the creative arts

(i)   The overall aim of this section, communication and the creative arts, is to develop the students' ability to communicate through speech, the written word, movement, music and through a variety of art forms.

(ii) Verbal communication is an integral part of all sections of the course. Language plays a vital role in the development of the young child. Students' ability to use and understand language is of paramount importance to their personal and professional future.

(iii) A wide selection of material should be presented to the students through personal contact with people, through the media of TV, radio, the theatre and cinema and tape recordings. These should be the avenue through which the students can be encouraged to read wisely, to listen carefully and to express themselves freely and accurately.

(iv) Many students will lack confidence in one aspect or other of the creative arts – it will therefore be necessary to create an environment in which students are stimulated to use their natural abilities; have the opportunity to develop a consciousness of quality of line, form, shape, texture, colour, sound, movement – and also see the importance of these for children.

b. Man and his environment

A study of 'man and his environment' should aim to give students some knowledge of man and of the interaction of man and his physical, biotic and economic environment.

It will be of paramount importance, in selecting out of a wide area of study, to choose themes and illustrations that have relevance to students in the modern adult world.

(i) Interdependence of living things — variety of life — care of living things, conservation, application of biology to agricultural and food problems.

(ii) Movement — characteristic of living things — large movements in nature — human problems in increased mobility. Biological consequences.

(iii) The continuity of life — inheritance — evolution.

(iv) Human biology, healthy living, etc.

(v) Material resources — trends — pressures — abuses — pollution.

c. Home and society

The aim of the study of home and society will be to obtain factual knowledge on how society has developed, is organised and sustained, to find out how to enjoy its benefits and serve its needs, and to examine the rights and responsibilities of the individual in relation to the home as a basic unit of society.

(i) The changing role of individuals in the family and society — the contributions that each member of the family can be expected to make — the skills and understanding that each must develop.

(ii) The likely pattern of family life. The need to establish priorities and the changing character of priorities. Home-making, recognising the changing needs of the family — developing some of the skills required for the good management of time, energy and money.

(iii) A realisation of the pressures on society. A study of human behaviour and human relationships. Attitudes to social problems such as old age, mental health, single parents, illegitimacy.

September 1976

Appendix B
Journals and Organisations

Journals

Child Education
Evans Brothers Ltd
Montague House
Russell Square
London WC1 5BX

International Journal of Early Childhood
World Organisation for Early Childhood Education
OMEP Publications
University College
Dublin 4

Mother and Baby
12 – 18 Paul Street
London EC2A 4JS

Newsletter and broadsheet
Centre for Information on Educational Disadvantage
11 Anson Road
Manchester M14 5BY

Nursery World with Maternal and Child Care
Bouverie Publishing Co Ltd
Cliffords Inn
Fetter Lane
London EC4A 1PJ

Under Fives and Community Relations
Community Relations Commission
15 – 16 Bedford Street
London WC2E 9HX

Organisations

British Association for Early Childhood Education
Montgomery Hall
Kennington Oval
London SE11 5SW

Church of England Children's Society
Old Town Hall
Kennington Road
London SE11 4QD

Doctor Barnardo's
Tanners Lane
Barkingside
Ilford
Essex IG6 1QG

National Association of Certificated Nursery Nurses
Secretary: Miss B. Gowan
158 Victoria Rise
Clapham
London SW4 ONW

National Association for Maternal and Child Welfare
1 South Audley Street
London W1Y 6JS

National Campaign for Nursery Education
33 High Street
London SW1V 1QJ

National Children's Bureau
8 Wakley Street
London EC1U 7QE

National Society of Children's Nurseries
Montgomery Hall
Kennington Oval
London SE11 5SW

Pre-School Play Groups Association
Alford House
Aveline Street
London SE11 5DH

Appendix C

Nursery Nursing Salaries — Negotiating Bodies

Nursery nurses employed by local authorities

National Joint Council for Local Authorities' Administrative, Professional, Technical and Clerical Services

Employers' Secretary
41 Belgrave Square
London SW1X 8N2

Staff Secretary
Nalgo House
8 Harewood Row
London NW1 6SQ

Nursery nurses employed by health authorities

Whitley Council Room 262
Hannibal House
Elephant and Castle
London SE1

Appendix D

Additional Training and Study for the Qualified Nursery Nurse

In-service courses

Once qualified, the nursery nurse will extend her knowledge and understanding through her work with young children.

When nursery nurses are employed by a large organisation it is not unusual for them to be offered in-service training courses of one kind or another. These courses are very varied in subject matter and length and will usually meet the local needs of the employers concerned; for example, an authority which had a high proportion of immigrant families might put on a special course for staff working with the young children from such families.

In-service courses are sometimes run as refresher courses to update the knowledge of nursery nurses who have been out of college for some time, or to help to promote additional understanding of the language needs of young children. Such courses take many forms. Nursery nurses are usually eager to participate and do so whenever possible.

There has recently been increasing concern, however, about the fact that some nursery nurses are working with children with special needs and they should have extra training for such work. More formal additional training arrangements are presently being considered and developed in the light of substantial evidence of the employment of nursery nurses in circumstances other than group care of normal healthy children.

The Advanced Certificate in Nursery Nursing

In February 1975, in response to demand from nursery nurses and some employers, the Board decided to develop opportunities for further study to a more advanced level in the care of young children.

The basic course leading to the NNEB Certificate is concerned with the study of patterns of normal development of children from birth to 7 years of age and the acquisition of skills of caring for young children in a group situation. But nursery nurses are now also to be found working with sick and handicapped children in hospitals, schools and day centres, and with severely deprived children in day/residential nurseries. The basic course does not and cannot equip students with the necessary knowledge and skills to meet the special needs of these children.

A course has therefore been developed leading to the Advanced Certificate of the NNEB. The aim of the course is to foster the personal development and professional confidence of experienced nursery nurses and to equip them with the knowledge and skills necessary for the day-to-day requirements of handicapped and deprived young children in a variety of settings.

The first pilot course leading to the Advanced Certificate was established at Bradford College in September 1976. The course is a full-time course, extending over an academic year and including practical and theoretical elements. For entry to the course candidates have to have the following qualifications and experience: 5 'O' levels or equivalent, an NNEB Certificate and three years' full-time post-qualification experience with young children. The course content is designed to offer additional knowledge and experience to the nursery nurse. Studies of the developing child are combined with study of the child in various handicapping situations. As well as special visits, a block practical placement is arranged for students, and this ties in with a special study which each student decides upon. The examination is by assessment and by consideration of this special study, which is between 7,000 and 9,000 words long. Three distinguished people have acted as external examiners in this initial pilot course, which has been considered very successful. It is hoped that a further pilot course will take place in September 1978 at Ipswich Civic College.

The Central Council for Education and Training in Social Work

The Central Council for Education and Training in Social Work (CCETSW) is an independent body, financed by the government, which has statutory authority throughout the United Kingdom to promote education and training in all fields of social work, to recognise courses and to award qualifications.

CCETSW is responsible for training staff of day, domiciliary, field and residential services of local authority social services/social work departments, social workers who work in the health service and social workers in education services, the probation and after-care service and voluntary organisations.

In December 1973 the Council accepted an invitation from the Department of Health and Social Security to develop education and training for those working in day care to include provision for further study for NNEB certificate holders employed in the personal social services. This has been taken into account in planning training for staff in residential homes and in day centres. The Certificate in Social Service is a new form of training being promoted by CCETSW for a range of persons already employed within the personal social services.

Recent developments in the personal social services have led to the recognition that additional skills are needed to provide support for families with young children and that nursery nurses, if they are to act as more than assistants, need to be released for courses leading to the Certificate in Social Service or the Certificate of Qualification in Social Work so that they can meet those new demands.

For further information about these courses nursery nurses should write to:

The Director
CCETSW Information Service
26 Bloomsbury Way
London WC1 2SR

Index